Motor Electrical Predictive Maintenance & Testing

Volume 2
Technologies for Motor Manufacturing and Repair

9th EDITION

By
Jack R. Nicholas, Jr., P.E., CMRP
Editor & Co-Author

Geoffery Generalovic
Co-Author

Contributors:

Noah Bethel, CMRP
Forrest Pardue
Dr. Greg Stone, PhD

Motor Electrical Predictive Maintenance & Testing

Volume 2
Technologies for Motor Manufacturing and Repair
9th EDITION

Jack R. Nicholas, Jr., P.E., CMRP
Editor & Co-Author

Geoffery Generalovic
Co-Author

Contributors:
Noah Bethel, CMRP
Forrest Pardue
Dr. Greg Stone, PhD

ISBN 978-0-9838741-1-9
HF082014

Publisher: Terrence O'Hanlon
Layout and design: Jenny Brunson
Cover design: Nicola Behr

For information: Reliabilityweb.com
www.Reliabilityweb.com
P.O. Box 60075, Ft. Myers FL 33906
Toll Free: 888-575-1245   Phone 239-333-2500
Email: customerservice@reliabilityweb.com

10   9   8   7   6   5   4   3

Copyrights and Disclaimer

Acknowledgements

Jack R. Nicholas, Jr., P.E., CMRP, a sole proprietor, was editor, author, and originator of all previous editions of this text. For this 9th Edition, he was joined by Geoffrey Generalovic of Hamilton, Ontario, Canada, as co-author.

The co-authors are grateful for support of the following companies and individuals who provided materials and granted permission for their use in this text and the seminars, web workshops and formal courses for which it was prepared.

> Dr. Howard Penrose, PhD CMRP, Manager of the ALLTEST Inc., at the time of his contribution to an earlier edition. Although the material is still used by ALLTEST, Dr. Penrose retains rights to use and/or donate its use to others. References to several other papers, articles and his book on motor circuit analysis appear in endnotes of several chapters.

> Mr. Don Ferree, Manager, EMPATH Sales AREVA NP, of Lynchburg, Virginia.

> Mr. Curt Lanham, President Baker Instrument Company of Fort Collins, Colorado, now a subsidiary of SKF Corporation - in 2004 authorized the use of the material attributed to Baker Instruments.

> Dr. Greg Stone, PhD, Vice President, Iris Power Engineering of Mississauga, Ontario, Canada, a subsidiary of Qualitrol Corporation., of Fairport NY, who made it possible for us to continue using much of the material on Partial Discharge in Chapter 11 of this text and also granted permission to continue using material from ADWEL.

> Mr. Noah Bethel CMRP, Vice President for Development, PdMA Corporation of Tampa, Florida who contributed his brilliant article on motor diagnostics using fault zone analysis and also contributed several case studies and individual images.

Mr. Forrest Pardue, President of 24/7 Systems Inc., who granted permission to use material in Chapter 13 on browser based motor data management.

Mr. Marton Dundics, President/CEO of The DEI Group of Millersville, Maryland, who as North American representative for Artesis, LLP, granted blanket permission to use the material on Motor Quality Monitoring and further provided information on the Bayesian Belief Networks.

The co-authors express their gratitude to Terrence O'Hanlon, Publisher, who had faith and vision to make this project into much more than just another massive black and white hard copy text but also dedicated the resources to provide it in four volumes with full color graphics and turn it into an e-book as well.

Last but not least, we thank Jenny Brunson, responsible for layout and design of new books at Reliabilityweb.com. Jenny patiently and professionally performed and oversaw the arduous work of converting the text into the four volume, hard copy and e-book formats.

Table of Contents

9th EDITION 2011

Volume 2

Technologies for Motor Manufacturing & Repair

Note: All four volumes have respective PowerPoint® slides in handout format in an Appendix C. All also have an identical Appendix D - Bibliography, and Appendix E - Index, unique to each volume. Volume 4 contains Appendix A - Article on Multi-Motor Refurbishment and Upgrade Project, and Appendix B - Audit Points for Visits to Motor Repair Shops.

Preface

This text has evolved significantly since it was first produced in the early 1990's. At first, developments in predictive maintenance, motor designs, repair techniques and materials for the electrical side of motors were developing so rapidly that updates were required every year or so. Now almost 20 years after the first text was printed, a 9th Edition is in print, six years since the last one. The pace of new developments has slowed somewhat, but the need for knowledge seems to have grown significantly. Information is out there in many forms and forums, now. This text attempts to concentrate pertinent parts of it and give users guidance on what are considered to be the most important things to understand about motors and their management, today.

For this edition, the author for all earlier editions, Jack Nicholas, invited Geoffrey Generalovic, of Hamilton, Ontario, Canada, to be co-author. Geoff is a mill-deck experienced electrician and predictive maintenance practitioner with a wealth of practical knowledge. His wisdom has been reflected in many parts of this text. This international co-authorship resulted from a long term business affiliation that grew into personal friendships between not only the co-authors but also their spouses, who supported the effort to produce this latest book with amazing patience.

The contents have changed from what was an assembly of PowerPoint® slides in the 8th Edition into a full blown text in the 9th. Updated slides have been included in an appendix. Between footnotes, end notes and the bibliography, there are a large number of references to articles, texts, blogs and Internet addresses for resources that anyone involved with managing any aspect of motor assets should refer to when contemplating starting a new or upgrading an existing motor management initiative.

This text is designed for use by technicians and their immediate supervisors, people with their hands on or very close to motors and the machines they drive. It is filled with photos, easy to understand (if sometimes rough) drawings and graphs. Chapters 1 through 4 (Volume 1) explain the theory of how motors work, how the most common motors found in commercial and industrial facilities are constructed, how they are characterized by their nameplate parameters and what vulnerabilities, failure modes and causes are most prevalent.

With fundamental knowledge of Volume 1 in hand, readers will find it easier to understand material in Chapters 5 through 12 (Volumes 2 and 3), which contain descriptions of common tests performed during motor manufacturing and repair and diagnostic tests and predictive tools available to detect early signs of degradation in service. Results from tests and predictive tools enable users to recommend timely action to attack problems before they become much more costly to resolve and to make informed, defendable recommendations on major repairs or replacement when that is the right thing to do.

Chapters 13 through 18 (in Volume 4) are aimed at those who are contemplating, starting or already engaged in some aspect of motor management. These chapters provide practical, proven ideas on how to design, support and defend programs, how to make them continually improve and how to justify and obtain resources needed to start and expand the effort while gaining full cooperation from many others in your organization who feel they have a stake in motor purchases, reliability, preventive maintenance, repair, operation, costs, profitability and/or mission success.

Jack R. Nicholas, Jr., P.E., CMRP
Co-author and Editor

CHAPTER 5

Surge and Surge Comparison Testing of Motors

Introduction - Surge testing has been in use for over 80 years, with one of the earliest test examples being the "Rylander Test" developed and patented in the mid-1920's[i]. It is done to test the condition of windings and their insulation systems in motors and other electrical apparatus. In motors this test detects turn-to-turn, coil-to-coil, phase-to-phase and phase-to-ground insulation defects as well as reversed coil connections that cannot be found as easily using other methods.

At first, testing was completely manual which required the operator to be the control circuit of the tester, so that any deteriorated, but still useable, motor winding coils detected by the test were not subject to more (voltage) stresses put on them by the surge tester itself. Training was paramount to ensure proper application of the test equipment. This was the case until the mid 1980's when the industry started to develop new testers using advances in electronics. These advances allowed the detection of many faults by evaluating changes in the circuit characteristics such as resistance, leakage current, polarization index (PI), voltage, dielectric absorption (DA), and frequency response. Trip circuits built into the electronic circuitry of testers shut down testing on deteriorated machines before more damage could occur. The surge tester of today is very portable due to the replacement of the heavy step-up transformer, needed to conduct the tests in the past, with light weight electronic solid state power supplies.

Surge Testing Principles – Surge testing is based on evaluating effects of insertion of high energy (low current) DC voltage pulses with fast rise times (decaying transient) into electrical coils. Coil types in motors include those in AC stators, wound rotors, DC motor armatures and fields and synchronous rotor poles. Once connected, the combination of the tester and the coil(s) under test form an electrical circuit with its own characteristics. The pulses between coil winding and test set are affected (dampened) by the impedance encountered in this 'circuit'. Then, using wave form analysis or "ringing" frequency analysis you can detect problems such as grounds, shorts, opens or reversed coils.

A single coil or winding made up of several coils can be examined at increasing voltage levels while looking for indication of a fault such as, turn-to-turn insulation damage, any shorts to ground, as well as improperly connected (reversed) coil(s).

The test wave form generated is observed on the tester oscilloscope screen (Cathode Ray Tube –CRT- on the older testers and now the latest Light Conducting Diode –LCD- types). The shape and stability of the waveform are used to determine condition of the circuit, which in field testing may include the cable runs to the motors as well as the winding of the motor. Electrical coils have very low resistance (which can be ignored in what follows) and a large Inductance (Symbol L for Inductance). Inductance is the property of an electric circuit where a change in an electric current through it induces an electromotive force (voltage) that opposes the change in current.

A surge tester generates a pulse that is inserted into the coils by "charging" a capacitor or capacitor-like electronic device (Symbol C for capacitance) with electrons. The test pulse from the capacitor circuit is inserted into the circuit containing the motor coil using some form of "switch". This forms what is called a "Bell Circuit," in electrical terms, where the pulse "ringing frequency" between the Capacitor in the tester and the coil in the motor can be determined.

Frequency of the "ringing" is determined by the following formula.

$$f = \frac{1}{2\pi LC}$$

If "L" of the coil changes because of a fault (e.g., short) the frequency (f) of the circuit between coil and tester changes, affecting the wave forms on the tester screen.

Figure 5-1 illustrates a simplified block diagram of a modern computer-aided surge tester connected to a motor or motor coil for analysis.

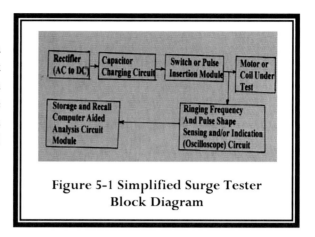

Figure 5-1 Simplified Surge Tester Block Diagram

The surge pulse distributes across coils being tested, so the peak and force is greater in the coils nearest the tester connection point than those further away.

Figure 5-2 shows the effect of different rise time pulses in a two pole, Wye connected, 6 turns per coil, 1000 Horsepower motor winding.[ii]

Pulses with shorter rise-times penetrate deeper into the winding coils. Pulses "stress-test" the insulation around the turns of a winding coil, but without hurting them, because current flow of the short pulses is quite low. Points where the insulation has

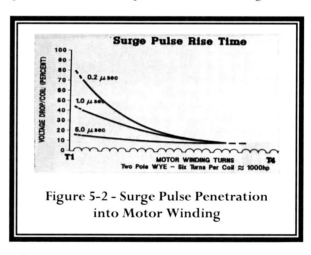

Figure 5-2 - Surge Pulse Penetration into Motor Winding

deteriorated will be revealed when arcing occurs between coil turns, to ground or between phases, simulating what happens in actual service.

Figure 5-3 shows an alternative image of pulses with the same rise times as those depicted in Figure 5-2. The point here is that current must change to cause the inductive effect. Longer rise time pulses allow inductive magnetic field induced "dampening" on current by the winding coils to then suppress the current. With a shorter rise time this dampening effect isn't as strong, allowing the voltage pulse to penetrate deeper into the winding before it dampens the changing current.

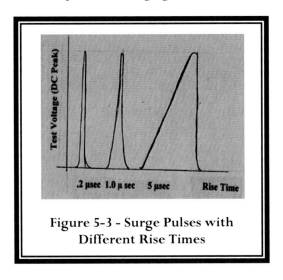

Figure 5-3 - Surge Pulses with Different Rise Times

Figure 5-4 illustrates two types of shorts detected by surge testing. Here there is a short between points 1 & 2 – Turn-to-turn – which deprives all turns between the two points of current, so there is no magnetic field from that part of coil that is "shorted". Short between points 3 & 4 – Phase-to-phase - diverts current and changes strength and shape of magnetic field from affected coils.[iii]

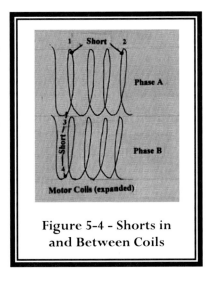

Figure 5-4 - Shorts in and Between Coils

Surge Comparison Testing of Motors - Surge comparison testing for poly-phase motors is based on the principle that if all of the motor's windings are intact and undamaged, then their electrical characteristics will be identical. For example each phase of a three phase motor is tested against the others. The instrument imposes a series of voltage pulses upon the winding phases in stages or steps of increasing magnitude. The final test voltage is determined by using the rated line voltage for the motor or coil being tested plus an additional amount to ensure the system still retains a "margin" to offset effects of aging over time. Electrical characteristics determined by the condition of all the connections and winding components that make up the circuit create what are called "ringing" pulses that are shown on the instrument's screen. If the two windings are identical in condition then the pulse images will be identical. If there is any shift or distortion in the pulses it indicates there are one or more problems with the winding. Today, to eliminate or minimize the chance of damaging coils or windings that are being subjected to test, current is limited by using a high frequency "pulsing" (15-200KHz) or oscillating voltage. Use is made of characteristic high "reactance" of winding coils as explained below. When there are voltage differences between adjacent conductors of a coil or coils, the voltage difference rises to a certain level (defined by a relationship called Paschen's Law), when arcing will occur through the damaged insulation.

Paschen's law requires a minimum 335 Volts for the test to produce arcing at atmospheric pressure.

The arcing occurs at the point of a "short" where current bypasses some number of turns in the same coil, flows between turns in separate coils or passes to ground. The arcing caused by the current flowing between turns is typically intermittent as repeated "pulses" are injected into the winding being tested. So any resulting wave form appears "collapsed and unstable".

When the surge test pulses cause arcing between turns of a coil or motor, the overall impedance of the circuit changes, with the biggest change in the inductance of the circuit (since the capacitance of the tester is constant – resistance of the circuit changes just a little bit and can be ignored). The ringing frequency of the circuit made up of the motor and tester changes (increases) so that on an oscilloscope, the effect is to shift the wave form to the left (closer to its origin on the screen). On an

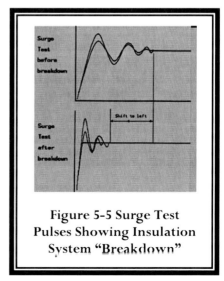

Figure 5-5 Surge Test Pulses Showing Insulation System "Breakdown"

undamped oscilloscope, the arcing creates the appearance of "flickering" "jitter" or instability. Figure 5-5 illustrates this "breakdown" indication.[iv]

Comparison is made between two or more "bell frequency" wave forms from motor coils or phases of a motor. When wave forms from the phases under test are viewed together they should appear to be identical, or close to it. This means the phases being tested have the same (or close to the same) electrical characteristics. If the wave forms are viewed together on a multi-trace oscilloscope and are moved so that one wave form overlaps the other, they should appear as one (or close to it). Any significant 'mismatch' indicates a difference in impedance, most likely due to difference in the inductive reactance of the phases under test.

Comparisons in three phase motors are made two at a time - Phases 1 to 2, 2 to 3 and 3 to 1. So the fault in one phase will be revealed by mismatched trace of the phase containing the fault compared to the 2 "good" phases. When coil or winding surge pulse characteristics are "compared" either to a "master" or to each other in a given unit or situation, "surge comparison" is occurring. If no master is available, tester operators revert to a straight "surge test," raising test voltage in steps to recommended limit or until the wave form collapses or becomes unstable. When that happens test voltage is removed immediately to preserve whatever life of the insulation is left and to prevent collateral damage.

Figure 5-6 illustrates some characteristic pulse shapes seen on surge tester screens for a machine in good condition and for three different types of faults seen in motors.[v]

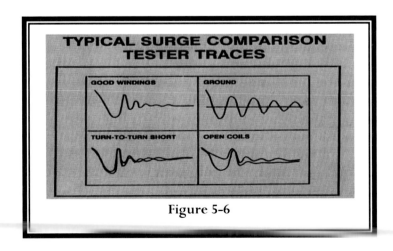

TYPICAL SURGE COMPARISON TESTER TRACES

GOOD WINDINGS GROUND

TURN-TO-TURN SHORT OPEN COILS

Figure 5-6

Analysts skilled in surge testing become familiar with oscilloscope wave forms and can tell from their characteristic shapes or "traces" the types of defects that are most likely present. Faults in single phase and DC motor components are revealed when mismatch occurs between the coil under test and a "master" known to be representative of a good winding or coil.

Modern surge testers have the capability of storing "known" wave forms and historical tests on the same motor. They can be compared, historical or comparison (Master) waveforms to the present wave forms, to see if there is any change or abnormality. This analysis method used to support conclusions is called "pattern recognition," discussed in more detail in Chapter 12 (Volume 3) of this text. All of the analysis is performed on a multi-trace Cathode Ray Tube (CRT) or Light Emitting Diode (LED) oscilloscope screen which displays the stored and newly acquired wave forms for comparison.

Surge testing is a valuable test during initial motor construction, motor rewind and when intermittent problems develop in a motor circuit. Surge and Surge Comparison Testing is one of few tests that can definitively indicate turn-to-turn or phase-to-phase shorts in motors.

The test can also be used in the field (using the modern, light weight testers available today) to perform motor circuit insulation system diagnostics.

Predictive analysis is also possible using the newer equipment with its ability to develop routes, store past tests results, compare tests and generate reports. Trends become very evident with this ability to store and compare data over time.

<u>Determination of Surge Test Voltage</u> -All insulation can be caused to fail if a high enough level of voltage is applied. With that in mind the person running the test has to assure that there is no risk to insulation when it is new and when it is in-service. Various authoritative sources of "standards" have established recommended levels for testing based on line voltage or nameplate voltage ratings of motors.

Some of the sources include:

- Institute of Electrical and Electronic Engineers (IEEE) Standard 95- Insulation Testing and IEEE 522- Surge Testing
- Electrical Apparatus Service Association – EASA

- IEC 34-15

Surge & Surge Comparison Testing - Max Voltage - New & In-service[vi] -

All standards recommend testing voltages for electrical components should be lowered from the values applied when new or before fully insulated. For in-service surge testing (and for testing coils before they are cured with insulating materials) authoritative guidelines are as follows.

- EASA, NEMA & IEC recommend 65% (.65) of test voltage when new.
- IEEE 522 Recommends 75% (.75) of test voltage when new.

In general, for all DC test voltages for motors (460 to 13,800 Volts AC) the formula 2E + 1000 Volts (E=Rated Volts (AC) in DC units – 1 for 1 AC to DC) gives a value that is:

- Aggressively high to slightly lower for low voltage motors
- Conservative to very conservative for high voltage motors

Surge (and DC High Potential) Testing Voltages – As indicated above, standards differ as to test voltage to use for surge (and DC High Potential) testing of AC machines. Something in between extremes would appear to be a prudent choice to use.

Per NEMA MG 1

Section 12.13 - Apply 1000 + 2 times Rated (Nameplate) Volts to new windings

Section 3.01 – Apply 75% of Volts (above) for in-service testing

Section 20.48 – DC Surge tester voltage = 1.7 times AC Voltage (AC to DC Energy Difference Factor)

Example for a 460 Volt AC Motor Using DC Tester

1000 + 2 x 460 Volts = 1920 Volts AC times .75 In-service factor = 1440 Volts (AC)

"Energy difference factor" times 1.7 AC to DC = 2448 Volts DC

2448 Volts DC is conservative compared to IEC standard, aggressive compared to IEEE 95 & 522.

Another example for a medium voltage motor typically found in utility plants appears below.

Per ANSI & IEEE Standard 95/2002

Section 5.1 - DC surge test voltage = 1.7 times calculated AC voltage using the 2E +1000 Volt formula

Section 5.2 - Maintenance proof testing should be performed using between 125% and 150% of rated Volts

Thus, for testing a 4160 Volt (AC) motor in service:

2 x 4160 + 1000 Volts = 9320 Volts (DC)

4160	4160	
x 1.25	x 1.5	125% to 150% Proof Test Factor
5200	6240	
x 1.7	x 1.7	AC to DC "Energy" Factor
8840	10,600 Volts (DC)	

9320 Volts is between the range of 125 and 150% recommended by IEEE 95

Surge Testing Considerations - The point of connection for the test leads will affect test results. For instance results for connection at the motor control center (MCC) will differ from test connection at the motor when it is disconnected from a circuit. The connecting or tester cables have all three factors of impedance present, which also have to be taken into account.

Rotor "coupling" or "rotor loading" will affect traces on the display screen of a tester, causing more rapid dampening and must be "cancelled" by positioning rotor or accounted for it if movement isn't possible. Traces from large AC motors with parallel connected winding coils are harder to interpret because of little or no trace separation (Inductance change is small relative to overall impedance of the winding). Traces from motors with a large number of coils in series are also hard to interpret. Small separations of "traces" on an oscilloscope are normal and generally no cause for alarm.

In wound rotor and synchronous machines lifting brushes and shorting slip rings is needed to cancel the "coupling" effect between stator and rotor windings. In AC & DC machines with multiple windings all but the winding under test should be grounded to eliminate inductive coupling effects. Equalized windings may affect wave traces but are ok if a "rhythmic shift" is observed as the armature is rotated.

Surge capacitors and capacitors for power factor correction must be disconnected from the motor circuit under test to avoid overloading the tester and suppressing the presence of faults, since the trace comparisons aren't as obvious.

When testing wound rotors and synchronous motor rotor field poles while installed, stator windings must be shorted and brushes lifted to prevent coupling effect and diode damage.

All windings and magnetic material close to coils under test must be the same for all so that a valid comparison can be made. For example, test all DC motor field poles of a motor while installed or all while on a bench alone, since coils differ in inductance due to different permeability between iron and air.[vii]

Surge Comparison Test Considerations[viii] - With the same number of coils and turns in each phase, Wye and Delta connected 3 phase motors will have different wave forms on the analysis oscilloscope. "Basket" or concentric wound motors have different lengths of magnet wire in the coils. There will be some small amount of separation between traces from each phase. As long as they are close in shape and very stable, there's nothing to be alarmed about. The same holds true for shunt coils in DC motors. When testing "chiller" or hermetically sealed motors, consultation with manufacturer's instructions is prudent to find what is needed to conduct a proper test (e.g., having to bring internal pressure to near atmospheric to avoid damage to the winding under test).

Surge testing is usually done second in sequence with Hi Pot testing, since the use of the Hi Pot test results are the upper limit for maximum voltage to apply during surge testing.

Surge testing may also be used with special test procedures on:

- Transformers
- Coil Heaters

Surge Test Risks to Motor Condition - Users and vendors have raised an issue of risk when using high voltage for testing, but over time this has become a non-issue, based on experience. There are no documented claims to the contrary and no legal claims for liability from users or owners upon surge test equipment vendors. This is mostly due to the use of electronic sensors and circuits coupled with the powerful computers of today making the testers extremely sensitive to changes in the circuit being tested. They will react quickly to minimize the potential of damage to the faulted area, if one is present.

Numerous users have employed this method for in-service testing for decades without apparent harm to any of the motors they have tested. Training is a significant factor in this equation, coupled with the knowledge that comes with experience. One cannot expect someone to pick up a tester and have them be an expert on what they are seeing in the circuits/motors being tested. The school of hard knocks and multiple tests make for a good motor test practitioner. The good ones are worth their weight in gold.

Consensus is that if the motor insulation is weak, it is far better to find the emerging problem during the test (which must be done while shut down) than in normal operation when other losses may occur. Nonetheless, contingency plans, such as having replacement motor on site and having personnel available to do the change-out quickly once the fault is discovered, need to be in place to minimize start-up delays, if the motor being tested is no longer serviceable.

In-service surge testing is conducted by insertion of multiple high voltage pulses at high frequency (and low current) over a total of only a few minutes per year. Surge testing doesn't raise the temperature of the motor during test and is far less a threat than over-voltage pulses from VFD's or from inductive load starts and stops that induce random and repeated voltage "spikes" on the supply busses many times each day. It has been proven in shop tests not to cause failure even when continued for days at a time at recommended maximum voltage level.

With its unique ability to find emerging turn-to-turn and phase-to-phase failures the relatively low risk of inducing a failure is more than offset by the benefit of avoiding failure during production. The unique feature of the surge test is its ability to find emerging winding failures at voltage levels well above alternative low voltage test methods (e.g., motor circuit analysis), providing added earlier warning than other test methods. When a failure does occur during production, surge testing can quickly reveal the cause, leading to an early decision on the type of repair needed.

Advanced Winding Surge, HiPot and Resistance Tester -

The newest Surge/HiPot testers are computerized marvels , capable of conducting a wide range of electrical tests and calculations, automatically. Once the testing is complete they are capable of storing test results for future reference, comparison of wave forms, trend analysis, comparing readings over time for multiple

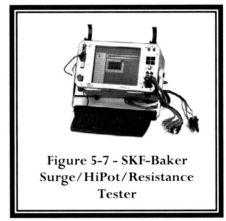

Figure 5-7 - SKF–Baker Surge/HiPot/Resistance Tester

machines and providing results for report creation. They can be set up for data collection on a route based format. Figure 5-7 shows a late model tester.[ix]

Case Studies Involving Surge Testing – There are situations encountered in failure analysis of motors that can't be readily solved with any other test method than surge testing. All of the case studies described below fall into this category.

Case Study #1 - A St. Johns River Power Park, Jacksonville, FL, 6900 Volt, 3 Phase, 600HP coal pulverizer motor tripped off line during a startup. Check for grounds with resistance-to-ground (RTG) meter at 1000 Volts DC showed no faults to ground, with readings acceptable. Motor restart was attempted, but it tripped again. This motor had been upgraded from 500 to 600HP and a new Class H insulation system installed 22 months before. The motor was returned to the shop where upgraded as it was still under warranty. Shop surge test showed insulation was breaking down at ~ 3800-4000 Volts of pulsed DC (which simulates AC without high current), far less than the rated AC voltage but much higher than detectable with the 1000 Volt resistance-to-ground tester at the plant. Ultimately the root cause was determined to be due to a lightning strike. See Chapter 16, Volume 4, for more details on this failure.

Case Study # 2 – A utility 4160 Volt 3 Phase pump motor circuit breaker tripped. Resistance-to-ground reading taken by plant personnel at 500 Volts DC showed a satisfactory reading. Conductor path resistance readings also showed no problem. Surge tester showed turn-to-turn fault at 500 Volts. This indicated that insulation breakdown was not complete until surge test pulsed DC voltage stressed the winding to the point where the fault was revealed.[x]

Case Study #3 – A chemical plant began initial surge testing of critical motors during plant shutdown immediately after receipt of their first tester. A 4160 Volt "stirring" motor inside a reactor vessel showed a turn-to-turn fault at 2000 Volts. Failure when motor was in service would have required 12 hours just to get inside the vessel, and the batch in process would have been ruined. Savings in this case exceeded cost of the tester[xi]. It should be noted that this could only be due to fortunate timing. Turn-to-turn shorts in medium and higher voltage motors normally progress to complete winding failure so quickly (days or hours from initiation) that the chance of finding one in progress is very limited.

Case Study # 4 – A Champion Paper Company 460 Volt, 3 Phase, 60HP motor was pulled for new bearings and other minor repairs. RTG showed "infinite." HiPot test to 2800 Volts DC was satisfactory. Surge test showed phase-to-phase fault at 650 Volts. Recommendation was to rewind because estimate was that it would only survive 2 or 3 more starts before failure. Because motor had run ok before removal, it was placed back into service without further repair. Motor failed during second start sequence after being reinstalled, shorted phase-to-phase[xii]. This was a judgment call based on the fact that such defects in low voltage motors can take months or years to develop to the point of failure.

[i] Rylander, J.L., Insulation Test Apparatus for High Frequency Voltage Discharge Patent # 3731185 can be seen at **http://www.freepatentsonline.com/3731185.html** and see R.L. Nailen, Electrical Apparatus Magazine 12/95.

[ii] Graph from paper by Christianson & Pedersen - Denmark IEEE 68C6-EI-87.

[iii] Figures 5-1, 5-3 and 5-4 were drawn by J, Nicholas.

[iv] Figure 5-5 was provided by R. Keith Young.

[v] Figure 5-6 is from U.S. Navy Basic Electricity Training Course Text NAVPERS 10086A.

[vi] Material and numbers used in the examples for test voltage calculations were provided in literature from Baker Instrument Co in 2003 and are used with permission of Curt Lanham, President at the time. AC to DC Energy Factor used (1.7) is from MG 1. Other sources provide values as low as 1.2 as a conversion factor. Also see www.pjelectronics.com website for an interesting discussion on the difference between what P J Electronics calls "Impulse" testing and what that company defines as true "Surge" testing.

[vii] Source for many of the considerations was Baker Instrument Company User's Manual 1/98 and interviews with test personnel in various motor repair shops.

[viii] Ibid.

[ix] Image from SKF Baker website.

[x] Source: Baker Inst Company Marketing Literature provided by Baker Instrument Company President Curt Lanham and used with permission.

[xi] Ibid.

[xii] Source: Plant Services Magazine 5/92 Reprint from Electrom Instruments Company.

CHAPTER 6

High Potential (Hi Pot), Resistance-to-Ground (RTG), Polarization Index Profiles (PIPs) and Diagnostic Tests[i]

Introduction – Insulation systems with all their various components and subsystems are vulnerable to many different failure mechanisms and causes. Tests for insulation system integrity are the most common conducted in many facilities. Most of these tests are performed with low cost instruments that do not create undue stress on the insulation, but do give good indication of whether or not it is deteriorating. By applying a voltage consistent with that normally present during operations and <u>for the right amount of time</u>, the instruments measure the amount of current that flows from the meter through the circuit being tested to ground and calculates and indicates the results in resistance terms such as megOhms (Millions of Ohms) or kiloOhms (thousands of Ohms). In most cases deterioration occurs at multiple locations in an insulation system. Numerous paths to ground are created when contaminants get into cracks in boundaries and cover the outside components of an insulation system. These multiple paths allow current to "leak" to ground, defeating the system function, which is to keep power flowing through protected conductors to where it can perform useful work. Ultimately, either the cumulative effect of all leakage paths or one dominant final major fault path in the system causes massive current flow to ground and a protective device to shut off power to the affected circuit. Over-currents are also present just after application of test voltage, but dissipate quickly as described in the section of this chapter on resistance-to-ground measurement.

Motor manufacturers and rebuilders have more powerful testers that provide the capability to stress insulation systems with higher voltage levels in order to determine what margin above every-day in-service conditions exists in an insulation system. These fall into the general category of high potential (HiPot) testers. These can measure and indicate very low levels of current passing from the tester through the insulation system under test to ground. Modern versions of HiPot testers have circuits designed to terminate testing when leakage current increases rapidly indicating imminent breakdown of an insulation system. This prevents further damage. Versions of these testers have been taken into the field for testing in-situ. Most are combined with surge testers by commercial vendors of test instruments.

Modern electronics and computers have been employed to provide more sophisticated ways of evaluating insulation system integrity. The methods used give earlier and more consistent indication of the onset of deteriorating conditions in systems. One of these, known as the Polarization Index Profile test (and by other names), will be described for use in the field as well as during motor repair and refurbishment in a shop.

Still, relatively simple diagnostic tests with simple tools can provide valuable information on where problems exist in machines undergoing investigation to determine what needs fixing. A few of these, done mostly in repair shops, but occasionally used in the field to localize and define the nature of problems are described in this chapter.

Finally, a brilliant approach to diagnosis of various "fault zones" in motor circuits is included to illustrate an experienced analyst's way of localizing and if possible pinpointing the nature of electrical and electro-mechanical problems commonly encountered.

<u>Insulation System High Potential (HiPot) Testing</u> – High potential (HiPot) or high voltage testing is performed in all motor manufacturing facilities and all motor repair shops. This test has been taken by some organizations to the field for use as an insulation system integrity evaluation tool. It is a fundamental motor industry acceptance test to assure insulation integrity. It is a simple, easy application of force (voltage) which is ideal for new and rewound motors.

Once a circuit to be tested is de-energized and proven safe, the motor winding must be isolated, frame grounded, and potential transformers and thermal sensors shorted or grounded.

A ramp or step method should be used to perform the test. Some testers do this automatically.

The actual test sequence takes 1 to 5 minutes. HiPot testing is a "test against a limit" as discussed in Chapter 12, Volume 3. A typical AC insulation system should be able to withstand at least 1.5 times rated voltage as discussed in Chapter 5 of this volume. DC systems often are tested by manufacturers and shops by application of the "2, 3, 4, 5" Rule, where "E" in the table below is voltage.

Rated Voltage (E) of Motor	Test Voltage
2300/4000/6900	2E
460	3E
230	4E
110	5E

Figure 6-1 shows a voltage vs. (leakage) current plot of an insulation system that has excellent integrity as indicated by the smooth curve with no insulation system "breakdown." The DC voltage (force) applied to "stress" the insulation system has been successfully withstood.

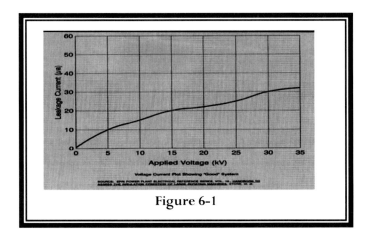

Figure 6-1

Figure 6-2 illustrates a typical plot of a HiPot test where a breakdown occurred before the voltage reached the predetermined limit for its termination. Such an effect may be anticipated particularly in DC HiPot testing, when and if the leakage current indication begins to show instability. In some designs to stabilize digital meter readings, the current sensor signal is dampened electronically. This obviates indications of instability.

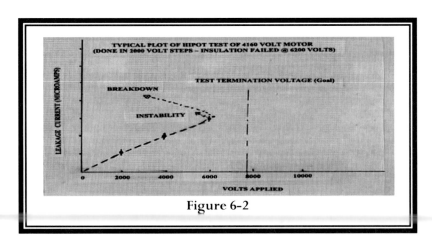

Figure 6-2

AC voltage HiPot testers are also available, but are not used as often because AC power signals contain much more energy and have some other shortfalls discussed below.

Testing During Rewind

Hi Pot testing is performed during motor component rewinding to see if coils might have been damaged during insertion into slots. It is performed on all AC & DC motor components at various stages of the rewind process. Figure 6-3 illustrates a typical test setup.

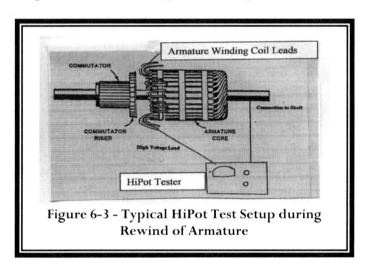

Figure 6-3 - Typical HiPot Test Setup during Rewind of Armature

Hi Pot Test Unit

Figure 6-4 shows an older Hi-Pot Tester has two controls & meters, one for voltage and the other for current. This is a perfectly useable instrument, but requires more operator attention than more modern ones.

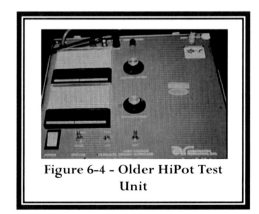

Figure 6-4 - Older HiPot Test Unit

Figure 6-5 show the presentation from a computerized Hi Pot tester as transferred to a larger screen monitor. Main readings are applied voltage and leakage current as seen on the right.

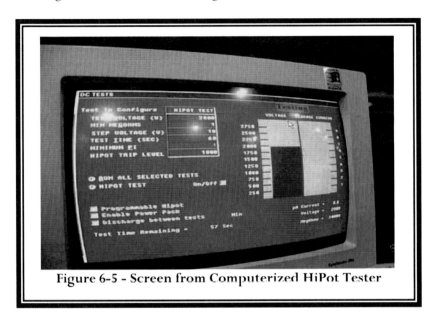

Figure 6-5 – Screen from Computerized HiPot Tester

Computer based HiPot testers, often combined with surge testing capability in the same unit, provide many advantages including storage, recall and analysis of results over time.

HiPot Test Risks to Motor Condition - Just as for surge testing (described in Chapter 5 of this volume) there was fear especially by motor owners that applying high voltage stress on motor electrical components would result in their failure. In fact Electric Power Research institute (EPRI) literature of 1980's directed at member utilities primarily tended to confirm the view that the test may be destructive. It is true that at some voltage all insulation systems will fail. However, experts now view HiPot testing as no threat to healthy insulation systems, given tests are properly conducted within the guidelines of various standards and guidelines available today. This is especially true when the testing stress is compared to threats from voltage spikes or surges on grid and from nearby busses and facilities, from Variable Speed Drives (VSDs) that aren't working properly and natural events (such as lightning) that occur frequently in some areas. The same recommendations and contingency planning described on Chapter 5 of this volume for surge testing apply also for HiPot testing.

DC rather than AC HiPot testing is recommended by EPRI and other authoritative organizations for the following reasons:

- DC gives earlier warning of instability than AC most of the time.

- AC Voltage can cause breakdown with very little warning, through this is not always true.

- Above 2300 Volts (@ 1 atmosphere pressure) AC can cause corona or partial discharge and rapid damage to insulation materials.

  ➤ This may not be a bad thing if you wish to prove these are present.

Case Studies Involving HiPot Testing[ii]

HiPot Case Study #1 – The Union Pacific Railroad routinely evaluates condition its fleet of DC traction motors on its engines using HiPot testing. These motors last a long time in service, with proper maintenance. One 750 HP, 30 year old motor was found during routine testing to have suffered a breakdown. Had the failure occurred in service with the engine hundreds of miles away trying to move a train of freight cars, the result would have been delays in movements that exceeded US$100,000.

HiPot Case Study # 2 - Ameren Central Illinois Public Service electric utility conducts routine HiPot testing of all critical motors on a regular basis. During one routine test a 4160 Volt, 3 Phase motor was found to have a breakdown at a voltage level well below the maximum recommended for testing at 2E +1000 = 9320 Volts. See Figure 6-6. Investigation revealed close proximity of a phase connection with severely

Figure 6-6 - Damaged Leads Can Ground a Motor Circuit

damaged insulation to the cover of the terminal box. Had this motor failed the plant was limited to 50% for a day and estimated replacement power cost was $643,288 per day.

Insulation Resistance-To-Ground (RTG) Testing –RTG measurements can be generally characterized as follows:

- It is the traditional method for insulation integrity measurement that uses simple, inexpensive test units with DC voltage output.
- Resistance relative to ground (nominal) is measured in Ohms (and indicated and recorded in kiloOhms [10^3 Ohms], megOhms [10^6 Ohms], or gigOhms [10^9 Ohms]).
- It gives overall indication of insulation condition (up to a point as described below).
- Its goal is to determine using Ohm's Law ($R = E/I$) measuring current "leaking" to ground (I) via multiple paths and voltage from the instrument (E) what the condition of the insulation system is in the circuit being evaluated.

IEEE Standard. 43-2000 is the latest version of the widely accepted standard that has been around since 1974. Among many other matters related to RTG tests and evaluation of results it provides guidelines for DC voltages to be applied during insulation resistance test. Some are provided in the table below.

Winding rated voltage (V)*	Insulation resistance test direct voltage
<1000	500
1000 – 2500	500 - 1000
2501 – 5000	1000 - 2500
5001 – 12,000	2500 - 5000
>12,000	5000 – 10,000

*Rated line-to-line voltage for 3 phase AC machines, line-to-ground voltage for 1-phase machines, and rated direct voltage for DC machines or field windings.

IEEE Standard. 43-2000 also provides recommended minimum insulation resistance @ 40 degrees Celsius (all values in megOhms) seen in the following table that are considered acceptable for the vast majority of insulation systems in use today.

Minimum Insulation Resistance (IR) (in megOhms)	Test specimen
$IR\ @\ 1\ minute = kV + 1$ $(megOhms)$ (where kV- kiloVolts is the rating [e.g., on the nameplate] of item under test)	For most windings made before about 1970, all field windings, and others not described below
$IR\ @\ 1\ minute = 100$ $(megOhms)$	For most DC armature and AC windings built after about 1970 (form-wound) coils
$IR\ @\ 1\ minute = 5\ (megOhms)$	For most machines with random-wound stator coils and form-wound coils rated below 1 kV.

The guidelines and values for RTG acceptance changed significantly from versions prior to year 2000. This was primarily to enhance personnel safety, and reflects the consensus of IEEE-43 Review Committee members that insulation system materials and application processes had changed for the better and permitted more stringent guidelines.

Resistance to Ground & Current Flows

Three or four things occur when DC Voltage is impressed on a motor winding insulation:

1. Capacitive charging current flows until the motor has reached its "capacity" to store electrons. This may take several minutes depending on the meter used and the system capacity.

2. Absorption current flows, but falls to zero in 1-2 minutes due to:

- Insulation component molecules being "polarized" by electrons and

- Drift current through molecular structure of the insulation materials.

3. Conduction current may flow, but is essentially zero unless moisture has saturated the materials, which is rare with todays non-hydroscopic Class F, H and higher temperature systems.

   - Older insulation systems have naturally higher conduction current.

4. Leakage current flows through multiple paths (such as cracks filled with conductive contaminants as successive heating and cooling occurs) in the insulation and over its surface (also contaminated with conductive substances over time) to some component such as a motor frame and thence to "ground".

   - This leakage current is what remains after all of the currents above stabilize and forms the basis for using Ohm's Law - $E = IR$ or for purposes of this measurement $R = E/I$

   - Overall resistance (R) to ground of a motor is determined by known or measured test instrument output (DC) Volts (E) applied by the instrument across from conductors of the machine to some "grounded" point outside the insulation divided by leakage current in Amperes (I) forced to flow from the tester and measured by it.

      ✓ Resistance-to-ground (RTG) meters measure voltage & current and indicate RTG.

Periodic RTG readings are illustrated in Figure 6-7.

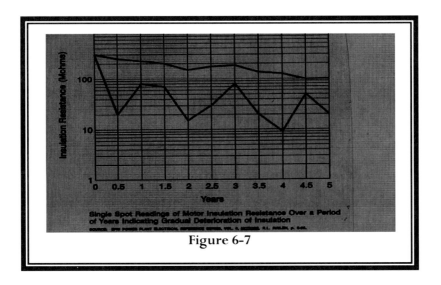

Single Spot Readings of Motor Insulation Resistance Over a Period of Years Indicating Gradual Deterioration of Insulation

Figure 6-7

- Temperature & humidity affect readings
- Lower curve = Raw data
- Upper curve is "normalized" to a common value temperature (typically 25 or 40°C), but never "normalized" for humidity. Data are then "trend analyzed." See Chapter 12, Volume 3, for more on trending.

Measuring Leakage Current

Progressive curves taken as a motor dries out are illustrated in Figure 6-8. Curve "A" shows a "wet" motor winding. Curve "E" is close to what is desired especially before adding any sealing insulation materials to those already in place. The section on Polarization Index Profiles later in this Chapter describes a similar but more definitive approach that can be done using readings taken both in the shop and in the field.

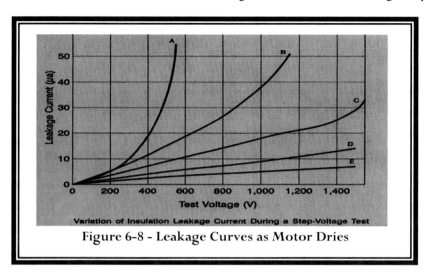

Figure 6-8 - Leakage Curves as Motor Dries

Insulation Materials and Temperature

A Rule of thumb is – for every 10° C increase RTG is halved. RTG has a "negative temperature coefficient" - the higher the temperature (e.g., in a motor), the less effective the insulation at performing its function of containing the power in conductors and directing it to where it can perform useful work. Figure 6-9 shows this for Class B insulation.

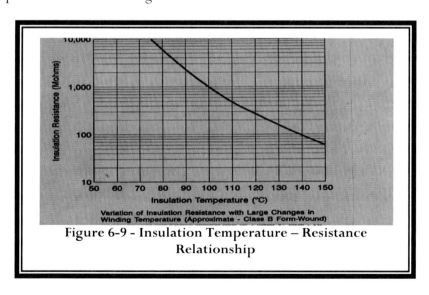

Figure 6-9 - Insulation Temperature – Resistance Relationship

Curves for classes F & H lay to the right and more or less parallel to the one in Figure 6-9.

Actual range of the negative temperature coefficient is ~ 8 C to 14°C for various classes to halve the RTG.

Experts such as those who prepared the latest update in IEEE-43 contend that RTG measured with DC voltage instruments provides only part of the assessment needed to understand true insulation system condition. A more accurate method would involve measurement of Impedance-to-ground (ZTG) where impedance has three components – resistance, inductive reactance and capacitive reactance. IEEE Standard 43 addresses these concerns and why the RTG has limitations.

In particular it points out that, whereas the AC voltage of a ZTG test, which has the capability to provide a measurement, one element of which (capacitive reactance - X_C) is sensitive to the presence of voids. To understand this you have to understand the impedance (Z) equation, one form of which is shown below.

$$Z = \sqrt{R^2 + (X_L^2 - X_C^2)}$$

Where Inductive reactance, $X_L = 2\pi f L$

and

Capacitive reactance, $X_C = \dfrac{1}{2\pi f C}$

f = frequency of the voltage imposed by the tester

If $f = 0$, then both X_L and $X_C = 0$ and $Z = R$

To measure Impedance-to-ground (ZTG) practically requires an AC voltage with a frequency high enough to provide a meaningful repeatable reading without high current flow. However, few ZTG instruments are used today, whereas millions of RTG measuring instruments are in constant use worldwide.

Ratios of Resistance-To-Ground

Over the years, ratios of RTG readings taken some minutes or seconds apart when voltage is applied continuously have been used as indicators of insulation system condition. These ratios may be of some value, but often are misleading for a variety of reasons.

If taken under the conditions recommended in IEEE-43 the following definitions and acceptance guidelines apply to use of RTG ratios:

- RTG @10 minutes divided by RTG @ 1 minute is called the Polarization Index (PI) Ratio.
  - ✓ If equal to or greater than two (2) for Class F or higher temperature class, it indicates the insulation system is OK.
  - ✓ If less than two (2) it indicates the insulation system may be deteriorating.

- RTG @ 1 minute divided by the RTG @ 30 seconds: is called the Dielectric Absorption (DA) Ratio
  - ✓ If near (or above) 1.5 it indicates that an insulation system is OK.
  - ✓ If less than 1.25 it indicates the insulation system may be deteriorating.

- The latest IEEE 43 says to ignore PI ratio if RTG is greater than 5000 megOhms after 1 minute and to use caution in comparing periodic measurements, unless taken under same conditions of temperature over the dew point.
  - ✓ Applies to motors of all sizes, but not to some types of motors like open winding machines.

- Best application requires a tester with upper range of 15 gigOhms [10^9 Ohms] or higher and measurements at the machine itself to avoid long cable runs from motor control centers that may have significant leakage currents caused by cable surface area.[iii]

Polarization Index Profile – PIP

When most measuring devices used for RTG measurement provide a reading, its value is "processed", averaged or dampened by internal circuitry so the readout instrument indicator (whether analog or digital) is stable enough for the human eye to interpret it. When placed on a graph these "stabilized" readings taken at 30 second or one minute intervals of continuous DC test voltage application produce a fairly smooth curve usually trending upward (as capacitive charging, insulation polarization and drift currents diminish). Computer aided testers can record multiple successive instantaneous readings with no damping needed. If such readings are taken three to five seconds apart and plotted, a whole new aspect of RTG evaluation (insulation system stability or instability) is made possible. If done for a total of 10 minutes, the normal time for developing what is called a Polarization Index (PI) curve or PI Profile (PIP), a weak insulation system will begin to show signs of its deterioration by PIP instability as illustrated in Figure 6-10.

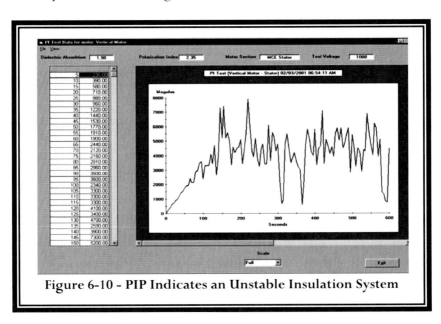

Figure 6-10 - PIP Indicates an Unstable Insulation System

The cause of the instability is the repeated buildup of electrons from the instrument attempting to measure RTG in the insulation system, over and above those that polarize the insulation material molecules, but related to the system capacity for storage or retention of electrons. Some leak paths have higher resistance or better conductivity than others and act somewhat like a "switch". That is, some paths are affected by the accumulation of charge from the electrons being stored there. When enough electrons build up, they cause these paths to "discharge" through the paths to ground in a "cascading effect." After the cascade of electrons the "switch" closes. The meter continues supplying electrons, again charging up the system and indicating that the RTG has suddenly dropped in value. In an undamped measuring device that is able to record instantaneous RTG readings rapidly, this build up and discharge effect is very obvious, repeatable and can be tracked through conditions such as progressive cleaning and drying cycles of a contaminated winding. The following case study illustrates this.

PIP Case Study #1 – Fuel Oil Service Pump # 3 motor at the JEA Northside Generating Station in Jacksonville Florida was placed in service after its last repair on 10/24/98. Baseline readings taken at the time included a PIP plot among many other readings. A year later during a routine PdM evaluation of condition, a PIP was recorded that showed significant instability in readings. The motor was removed to a local repair facility where it was opened and the winding found to be badly contaminated with oil soaked dirt. The winding was then cleaned and another PIP plot recorded showing most of the instability was gone, but readings weren't quite as high at the end as the year before. The winding was "dipped" in a compatible insulating "varnish" solution and the added insulation cured. A new PIP was almost identical to the one a year before.

Figure 6-11 shows the sequence of plots.

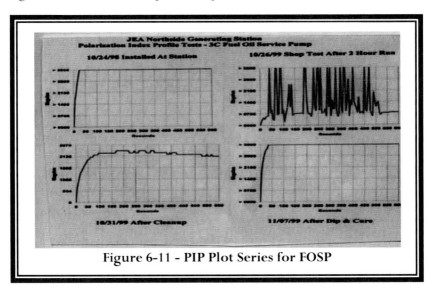

Figure 6-11 - PIP Plot Series for FOSP

PIP Case Study # 2[iv] - Figure 6-12 shows PIP plots for two identical 400HP 460 Volt motors in a merchant utility plant. One has a very unstable characteristic that didn't show up until half way through the test. The other has a lower initial RTG which gets better in the end. PI ratios are respectively 1.0 and 1.5. If faced with a choice of which to rely on, which would you choose?

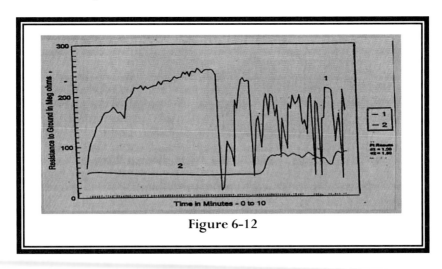

Figure 6-12

PIP Case Study # 3[v] - Figure 6-13 shows PIP plots for four identical 400HP 460 Volt motors in the same merchant utility generating plant taken on the same rainy day in February 1996. Note that two PI ratios don't meet the IEEE Standard 42 criteria for acceptance on this day. PIPs on the same motors on a dry day a month later in Figure 6-14 show all PI ratios meet minimum.

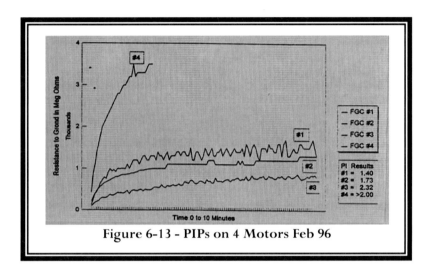

Figure 6-13 - PIPs on 4 Motors Feb 96

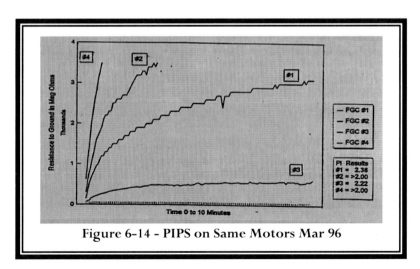

Figure 6-14 - PIPS on Same Motors Mar 96

PIP Case Study #4[vi] - A 400 Horsepower, 460 Volt, AC Induction, inverter duty, bag house fan motor had suffered four (4) Variable Speed Drive (VSD) failures within 3 years. VSD's were always replaced with new components at a cost of $45,000 each. After the last VSD replacement the motor was refurbished, but after hookup in the circuit, initial RTG reading was only 145 megOhms. All other circuit data were in the normal range. Between VSD replacements frequent trips of the motor were causing additional process problems. A PIP plot at a disconnect near the motor showed some instability, and final RTG of only 400 megOhms, indicative of moisture or other contamination somewhere in the circuit. The motor PIP plot showed some instability, but much higher final RTG. See Figures 6-15, 6-16 and 6-17.

Figure 6- 15 - Bag House Fan Assembly

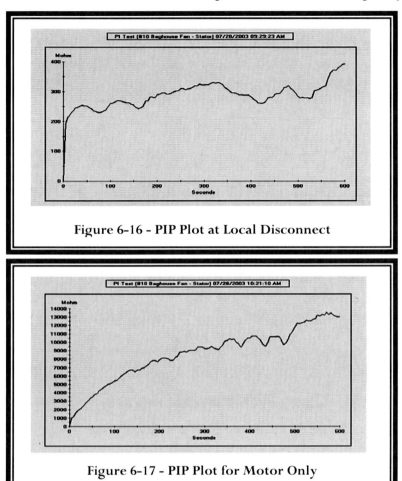

Figure 6-16 - PIP Plot at Local Disconnect

Figure 6-17 - PIP Plot for Motor Only

With motor RTG high and circuit RTG much lower, a problem was suspected between local disconnect and the motor connection box. The conduit was inspected for signs of moisture, but none was found initially. Due to some abrasions on lead-wire jacket, it was decided to have it replaced. As old wire was removed, water began leaking from jacket around it as shown in Figure 6-18.

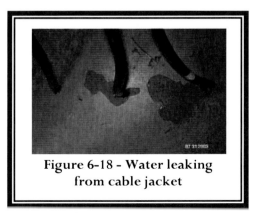

Figure 6-18 - Water leaking from cable jacket

PIP Case Study #5[vii] – A PIP Plot for a 75 HP DC Armature circuit is shown in Figure 6-19. RTG varies from zero to 3500 megOhms, the limit of this particular test suite at the time. At 1 minute into the test the RTG is at maximum. So, under IEEE Standard 43 guidelines this motor would pass with flying colors. However the rest of the plot shows severe instability. The motor was removed to a repair shop where it was cleaned, dried, dipped and baked. Post repair PIP plot showed stable maximum RTG readings throughout the duration of the 10 minute test.

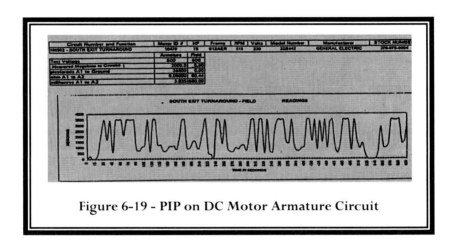

Figure 6-19 – PIP on DC Motor Armature Circuit

Use of Step Voltage to Find Insulation Problems - Step Voltage or Leakage Current vs. Voltage testing of insulation systems is a process of applying a series of successively higher DC test voltages, each for a specific period of time, usually 60 seconds, and recording the leakage current at the end of each period. The levels and step (increases) in voltage applied and the amount of allowable leakage current are set prior to beginning the test. Maximum voltage applied during the test is discussed in Chapter 5 of this volume. Effects of moisture, contaminants and damage to the insulation are usually revealed at voltages below those expected in service. However, the effects of aging or mechanical damage in fairly clean and dry insulation may not always be revealed at low voltage levels.

Advanced testers reach the teraOhms range, 10^{12} or 1 million million ohms. The newer tester capabilities and computerized data collection have given the technician the ability to evaluate motor insulation systems more carefully than ever before in the field. These advancements in data collection provide legitimate repeatable data that can be recorded and used for trend evaluation.

Figure 6-20 shows a typical step voltage test record for a good insulation system in a stator of a 4160 Volt motor, with micro-amps leakage current versus voltage in the graph to the left and micro-amps leakage current versus time on the right. Voltage is raised in 500 Volt steps from 1000 to 5000 Volts.

Figure 6-21 shows an insulation system of a stator that exhibits breakdown as voltage reaches just 1000 volts, well below the 5000 volt termination voltage.

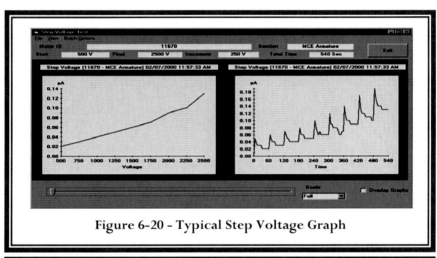

Figure 6-20 - Typical Step Voltage Graph

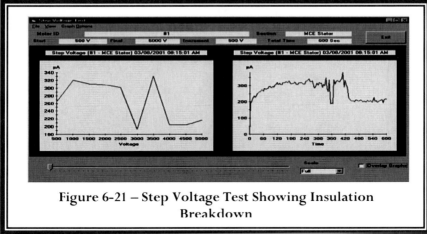

Figure 6-21 – Step Voltage Test Showing Insulation Breakdown

Figure 6-22 shows burned insulation in a 4160 Volt motor. It has been "Carbonized" making it conductive and allowing current "leakage" directly to motor frame components in contact with "ground" potential.

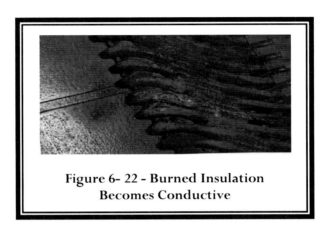

**Figure 6- 22 - Burned Insulation
Becomes Conductive**

Diagnostic Testing Using Light, Ammeter, Voltage Drop and Resistance Bar-to-Bar - Whether in the field or shop, troubleshooting may be employed to locate and confirm conditions in motors that need corrective action. Some troubleshooting tools are very simple – a light probe or ammeter connected to a power source and neutral to motor frame (which in turn must be solidly connected to ground for safety).

Troubleshooting Dual Voltage Motors with a Light Probe – See Figure 6-23.

- To find grounds, attach neutral of 120 volt AC power source to the frame and line probe to one end of each sector – Light indicates ground in that sector.
- To find opens, attach neutral & line probe to opposite ends of each sector – No light when open in that sector.

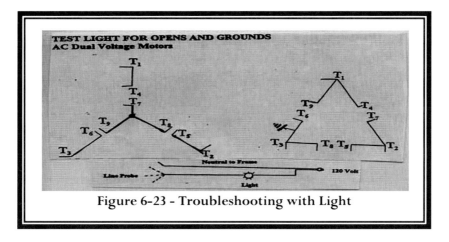

Figure 6-23 - Troubleshooting with Light

Troubleshooting a Compound DC Motor With a Light Probe –

See Figure 6-24. You must disconnect various circuits (series field S1 –S2, shunt field F1-F2 and armature A1-A2 which includes interpoles) for tests with a light probe to localize grounds in DC motors. With neutral of the 120 Volt AC line attached to the motor frame (which must also be attached to ground), touching the probe to any grounded circuit will turn on the light.

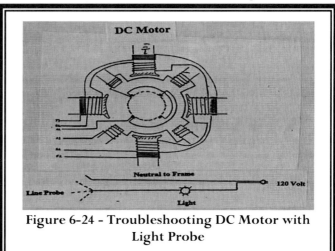

Figure 6-24 - Troubleshooting DC Motor with Light Probe

Connecting the neutral to each circuit #2 terminal and the probe to the #1 terminal will light the bulb, unless the circuit has an open in it. Further disconnection in the grounded or open circuit is then needed to find the faulty component.

Troubleshooting With an Ammeter Quantitative current data allows localization of ground. To perform these tests obtain a test signal from a power source and insert an ammeter between source and probe. Provide a return lead to the source from the motor frame.

In Figure 6-25, connecting the probe to point "A," which is closest to the grounded coil will provide a higher current flow then when connected to Points "B" or "C."

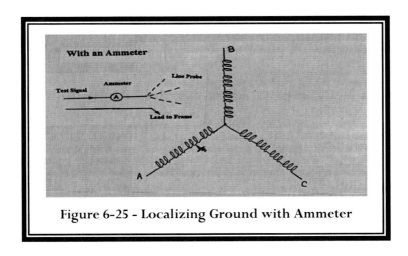

Figure 6-25 - Localizing Ground with Ammeter

It is harder to localize grounds in delta configured windings because current differences aren't as great due to multiple flow paths.

Voltage Drop Test - This test may be used on DC motor field circuits or AC Synchronous motor rotors to find poles that are shorted. The decision to rewind or do minor repair depends on location of short, age of winding and time available before motor must be returned to service. Either AC or DC voltage may be used, but AC gives the best indication (highest voltage drop per pole) with a small total voltage applied (~120 Volts in most cases). To perform this test on a synchronous machine such as that shown in Figure 6-26:

- Apply 120 V (AC) between slip rings
- Measure voltage between:
  - A & B
  - B & C
  - C & D
  - D & E
- Pole with lowest voltage drop is weakest (worst short)

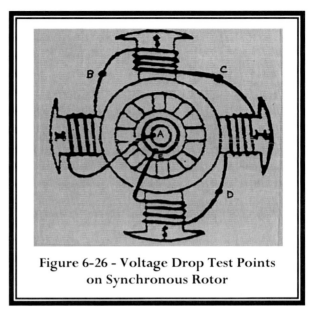

Figure 6-26 - Voltage Drop Test Points on Synchronous Rotor

- If all drops are equal, it indicates the rotor poles are in good condition

DC armatures suspected of having one or more coils shorted can be thoroughly tested using a quantitative bar-to-bar test.

- The test consists of using a milliOhm or microOhm meter to measure the resistance of each coil
- To obtain accurate readings, especially on large armatures where the resistance is quite low a special "four point probe" technique is used to eliminate effects of the resistance at the contact points of the probes on each bar
- All readings should be within about 10% of each other

In evaluating condition of very low resistance circuits such as those in properly connected armatures special probes called Kevin or four terminal probes are used. Figure 6-27 illustrates a set of these probes in use measuring resistance of armature circuits bar-to-bar on an 8000HP DC armature to determine extent of damage after a ground fault tripped the motor off line.

**Figure 6-27 –
Kelvin (Four point)
Probes Used to Measure
Low Resistance Circuits
Such as Bar-to-Bar on a
Large Armature**

Figure 6-28 illustrates how current is supplied via a pair of **force** connections (current leads 1 & 4). These generate a voltage drop across the impedance to be measured according to Ohm's law $V=IR$. This current also generates a voltage drop across the force wires themselves. To avoid including that in the measurement, a pair of **sense** connections (voltage leads 2 & 3) are made immediately adjacent to the target impedance. The accuracy of the technique comes from the fact that almost no current flows in the sense wires, so the voltages drop $V=IR$ is extremely low. Figure 6-29 shows how measurements from the armature shown in Figure 6-27 were charted,

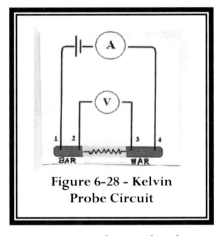

**Figure 6-28 - Kelvin
Probe Circuit**

defining the extent of the damage to armature winding and indicating replacing only these coils would allow it to return to service if necessary. Spikes indicate that armature coils between about 100 & 112 are damaged. Ultimately a replacement was installed and the damaged armature was completely rewound for use as spare.

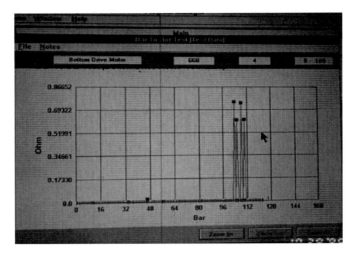

Figure 6-29 Bar-to-Bar Resistance

Identifying Motor Defects Through Fault Zone Analysis[1] - Putting it all together with a comprehensive approach to diagnostic testing and analysis.

The six electric Fault Zones are:

1. Power Quality

2. Power Circuit

3. Insulation

4. Stator

5. Rotor

6. Air Gap

---

[1] The remainder of this chapter consists of a shortened and slightly modified version of a paper by Noah Bethel, CMRP, Vice President for Product Development at PdMA Corporation in Tampa, Florida and is used with his permission. In the opinion of the co-authors it most accurately presents a comprehensive approach to troubleshooting motor circuits which should be adopted by all who are involved with diagnosis of motor problems.

Fault Zone 1 - Power Quality has recently been thrust in the limelight by utility deregulation and the popularity of AC and DC drives. With deregulation, competition among utilities has heightened the concern about penalties from high distortion levels. The variable speed drives (VSD's) and other non-linear loads can significantly increase the distortion levels of voltage and current. How can this distortion be minimized? What equipment is required, and is the concern purely financial or is equipment at risk?

First, let's understand what we are really talking about when we speak of power quality problems. Voltage and current harmonic distortion, voltage spikes, voltage unbalance and power factor are a few of the many concerns when discussing power quality. Although all of these are important, we will focus on just a few, beginning with harmonic distortion.

Distortion sounds like an in-depth concept. It becomes more elementary if you break it down to basic terms. Total Harmonic Distortion (THD) is the ratio of the root-mean-square (RMS) of the harmonic content of a power signal to the RMS value of the fundamental quantity, expressed as a percent of the fundamental. Quite simply it is the RMS value of the signal with the line frequency (fundamental) removed. A perfect 60 Hz sine wave would have 0% THD. So anything other than the fundamental line frequency (60 Hz) would be considered a harmonic distortion. Distortion makes a smooth fundamental sine wave signal into a ragged wave form with many positive and negative peaks and depressions. This causes magnetic fields of a motor equally distorted and non-uniform, creating havoc with motor action.

Common non-linear (switching) loads include computers, florescent lighting and variable speed drives (VSD's) as mentioned previously. The presence of harmonics in a distribution system results in excessive heat from the increased current demands. A load designed to pull 100 amps at full load may draw 120 amps if the harmonic distortion is high. This additional current can lead to insulation damage and possibly a catastrophic failure. Excessive zero sequence harmonics will collect back at the transformer, leading to overload and possible failure. These high zero sequence currents return to the source through the neutral bus, and, if excessive, can generate substantial heat and even fires. In an effort to avoid such catastrophic events, many companies are modifying their distribution systems. Installing k-transformers, designed to handle the larger loads generated by harmonics, and increasing the size and current carrying capacity of their Wye-connected motor neutral to motor control center (MCC) cable leads are two popular remedies. Though these efforts do nothing to diminish the harmonics, they do reduce the failure risk. Removing the harmonics requires the installation of filtering mechanisms, such as zero sequence filters.

Some of the newer VSDs that utilize IGBTs can exceed line voltage by a tremendous amount in less than a microsecond. Older Class B insulation systems have low tolerance for this rapid rise time and can fail very quickly. Motors designed for inverter duty are highly recommended when utilizing drives. Excessive cable length between the drive and the motor can create a high impedance mismatch that contributes to high voltage spikes at the motor connection box. The drive manufacturer will normally specify the correct cable distance (maximum recommended).

General guidelines as stated in Table 3.3.1 of IEEE Standard 519-1992, recommend less than 5% voltage THD for systems operating at less than 69 kiloVolts. They further recommend the individual harmonic voltage distortion to be less than 3%. Figure 6-30 shows an example of unacceptable levels of voltage distortion. (See Chapter 4, Volume 1, on other aspects of harmonics in motors.)

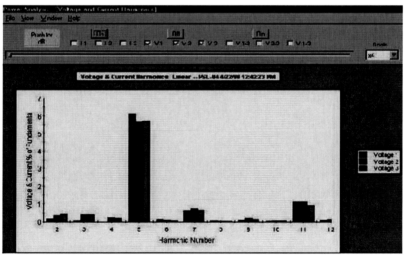

Figure 6-30

High 5th and 7th harmonics indicate the presence of a 6 pulse drive influence on the distribution system. Each of the individual harmonics should be less than 3% of the fundamental per IEEE Standard 519-1992.

Figure 6-31 shows a fundamental 60 Hz voltage signal with 6 pulses occurring throughout each sine wave. This resulted from an unfiltered 6 pulse drive connected to the distribution system.

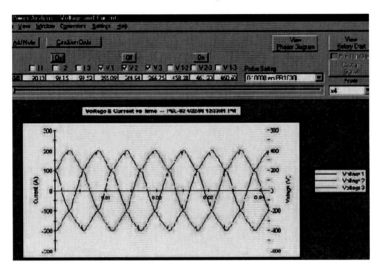

Figure 6-31 – Voltage Signal with 6 Pulse Distortions from VSD

Fault Zone 2 - Power Circuit: The power circuit refers to all the conductors and connections that exist from the point at which the testing starts through to the connections at the motor. This can include circuit breakers, fuses, contactors, overloads, disconnects and lug connections. A 1994 demonstration project on industrial power distribution systems found that connectors and conductors were the source of 46% of the faults reducing motor efficiency. Many times a motor, although initially in perfect health, is installed into a faulty power circuit with problems like harmonics, voltage imbalances, current imbalances, etc. As these problems become more severe, the horsepower rating of your motor should be reduced or temperatures will begin to increase and insulation damage begin to occur. If the motor is replaced without correcting the power circuit defects, the failure cycle will begin again.

As seen in Figure 6-32[viii], high resistance connections resulting in voltage imbalances will mandate reducing the horsepower rating significantly.

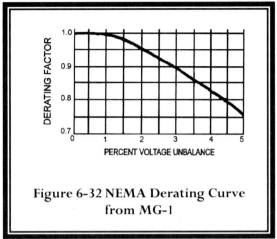

Figure 6-32 NEMA Derating Curve from MG-1

One method of detecting high resistance connections is by performing phase to phase resistance testing. On a three phase motor, the three resistance measurements should be nearly identical. If all three reading are exactly the same, there would be a 0% resistive imbalance. As one or more phases develop a high resistance the resistive imbalance increases, indicating a fault. Some of the fault mechanisms that cause high resistance connections are:

Corroded terminals   Loose cables
Loose bus bars   Corroded fuse clips
Corroded contacts   Open leads
Different size conductors   Dissimilar metals

Figure 6-33 shows three different resistance test points which can be used to determine actual location of the high resistance connection. Position X is upstream of the fuses. If the resistive imbalance is still high, you may want to move to position Y, downstream of the contactor. If the unbalance is still evident at position Y, testing at the motor connection box, position Z, will determine which is the power circuit problem area.

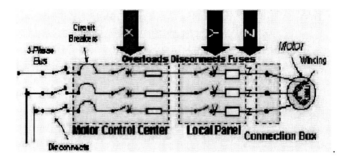

Figure 6-33 Test Points in Motor Circuit for Finding High Resistance Connections

Fault Zone 3 - Insulation: This refers to the insulation system between the winding conductors and ground. High temperatures, age, moisture, and dirt contamination all lead to shortened insulation life. It has been said that if plants would just use the space heaters available to keep the insulation dry, then doubling the life of our motors would not be out of the question.

Insulation systems today are better than ever and are able to handle higher and higher temperatures without significant reduction in life. However, we are still finding ways to destroy our insulation much earlier than should be expected. Keep in mind that although insulation is many times involved in a failure, this fault zone is heavily influenced by other problems. The power circuit for one can heavily influence the insulation. If a high resistance connection exists upstream of the motor which develops better than a 5% voltage imbalance, and we continue to run the motor at its normal HP rating, we will see a shortened insulation life. Reverse sequence currents developing rotating magnetic fields in the opposite direction will not only reduce the torque capability, but can allow the temperature to rise out of control and exceed even the 155°C limit on your Class F insulation systems. We also overload and thus overheat motors during operation and believe this is ok. It is easy to diagnose the evident insulation failure as the fault mechanism, but it will happen again with a different motor if problems are not fixed.

Again, testing with a RTG tester is not going to tell you everything, but it is a good start when it comes to insulation testing. Something that people often overlook when it comes to the IEEE (Institute of Electrical and

Electronic Engineers) minimums on resistance to ground is the reference to 40°C. As shown in Figure 6-34 simple RTG testing with no regard to temperature will result in resistance to ground readings which swing heavily from high to low, depending on the temperature of the windings. Temperature correcting the readings will not only meet the IEEE testing guidelines, it will give a much better trend as seen in the lower line in insulation RTG graph in Figure 6-34. (See Chapter 4, Volume 1, describing many other causes of insulation failure).

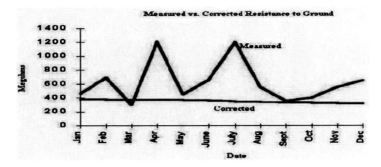

Figure 6-34 – Measured and Temperature Corrected RTG Readings over Time

We must realize that moisture contamination may cause the temperature corrected reading to be invalid. Ensure the heaters are energized when the motor is not running to prevent this from happening.

An insulation test that has fallen out of the spotlight is the Polarization Index test. Applying a constant DC voltage, in the form of a RTG tester test, for a period of 10 minutes will (in an insulation system in good condition) result in a gradual increase in the resistance to ground (RTG) reading. This is largely a result of "charging" the motor to its "capacity" to hold electrons, much like is done in charging a capacitor, and absorption current trailing off as insulation system molecules become "polarized".

Per ohms law, I (current) = V (voltage) / R (resistance)

Therefore, the reduction of this current must result in an increase in the indicated resistance. If we take the ten minute RTG and divide it by the one minute RTG, a value of 2.0 or higher is considered acceptable by IEEE. Unfortunately, motors with unstable insulation systems can give values close to or greater then a 2.0, but still be defective.

In Figure 6-35, when the ten minute reading (approximately 600 megOhms) is divided by the one minute reading (approximately 309 megOhms), the result is a PI of 1.94. This nearly meets the IEEE guideline for acceptance as a good insulation system, and would probably be accepted in the field. You can see, however, that this insulation system is very unstable. Always look at the Polarization Index Profile and not just the Polarization Index ratio.

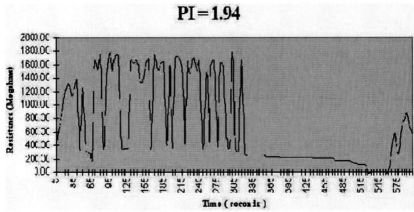

Figure 6-35 – Polarization Index Profile (PIP) Plot

A limiting factor about DC resistance to ground testing is that the DC signal will many times not give the best evaluation of the true insulation condition. The insulation on a motor is a natural dielectric material. Therefore it is a poor conductor of DC. This is good because you don't want excessive leakage to ground, but bad in that an insulation system in a degraded condition may take a bit longer to be identified using a DC signal or RTG tester. AC signals, however, do not allow the dielectric to charge and will pass through the dielectric much easier. This is good because it allows the use of an AC signal to give much earlier indications of insulation degradation, and bad because it can be destructive at some level, as with DC Hi-Pot tests. Low voltage capacitance-to-ground tests, however, are non destructive and very good early indicators of some degradation modes such as voids and contamination in or covering surfaces of insulation systems. These values will be read in pico-Farads (pF) and can be effectively trended over time.

Fault Zone 4 - Stator: When we mention the stator, we are referencing DC field or AC windings, insulation between the turns of the windings, the stator or field pole core laminations and solder or brazed joints in conductors between the coils.

One of the common faults occurring with motor windings is a turn-to-turn fault. This occurs when the insulation between two or more turns in the same coil breaks down and reduces the coil's ability to produce a balanced magnetic field. Unbalanced magnetic fields result in vibration, which can then cause degradation of the insulation as well as bearing failures. Localized heating around the short can also spread to other coils, resulting in a coil-to-coil short. Excessive heating will eventually not only destroy the motor winding effectiveness, but will also damage the insulation between the laminations of the stator core.

Another fault that can occur with multi-phase AC motor windings is a phase-to-phase fault. This results from the insulation breaking down between two separate phases, usually lying adjacent to each other in the same AC stator slot. A higher difference in voltage potential tends to make this fault accelerate very quickly. Slot paper is installed between different phases in the same slot to reduce the opportunity for leakage between phases.

A turn-to-turn or a phase-to-phase short can occur many times without resulting in an immediate ground fault. Because of this, testing with just a RTG tester for preventive maintenance or following a motor trip may not identify the fault. This could allow a small, undetected winding fault to develop into a major catastrophic failure. Permanent core damage may necessitate having to replace the core or even replacing an entire motor.

Testing of a stator can be done by connecting directly at the motor as well as connecting at the MCC. During the test, high frequency AC signals are sent into the motor. These signals produce magnetic fields around the windings which should be matched between phases. The inductance measurement for each phase is then compared to the other phases and combined for calculation of inductive imbalance. This imbalance minus the influence of the rotor is used to compare the ability of each of the phases to produce a balanced magnetic field. In a DC motor a voltage drop test described earlier in this chapter may be used to find faulty field coils.

Also during a test, DC signals are sent into the motor. From these signals the actual resistance of the winding or windings is measured. The three resistance readings of a three phase induction motor are compared and combined to produce a resistive imbalance. If this imbalance exceeds a predetermined level, then high resistance connections may exist in the solder joints between coils.

There are two basic types of stator winding configurations. The first is wye (or "Y") connected and the second is delta connected. To more fully understand what the inductance readings are telling you, a simple understanding of the winding configuration can help. Figures 6-36 and 6-37 show this concept.

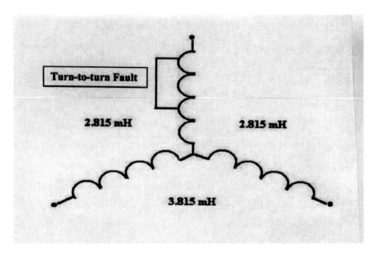

Figure 6-36 - Wye Connected Stator with Imbalanced Inductance

A "Y" configuration winding with a turn to turn short will result in two low inductance readings and one high inductance reading, when looking at phase to phase inductance.

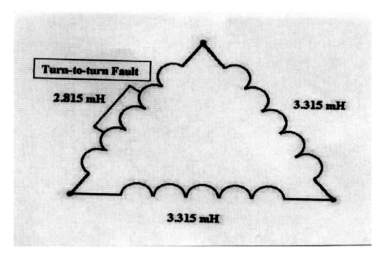

Figure 6-37 Delta Connected Stator with Imbalanced Inductance

A delta configuration winding with a turn to turn short will result in one low inductance reading and two high inductance readings, when looking at phase to phase inductance. For more on inductive imbalance see Chapter 7 of this volume.

Fault Zone 5 - Rotor: This refers to the rotor bars, the rotor laminations, and the end rings of the rotor. A 1980's study sponsored by EPRI and performed by General Electric Corporation showed that 10% of failures were found in rotors of utility motors[ix]. Other studies revealed about the same results. The rotor, although suffering a small percentage of the motor problems, can influence other fault zones. When a motor is started with a broken or cracked rotor bar or end ring, intense heat is generated around the vicinity of the break. This can spread to other parts of the rotor and destroy the insulation around nearby laminations. It can also affect other parts of the motor. The stator is just a few millimeters away from the rotor. Stator insulation cannot hold up to the intense heat developed by the rotor damage and will eventually fail. Unfortunately, many times broken rotor bars are not easily seen without use of tests with technologies described below and in other parts of this text, and it may be missed as the root cause of failures. This will result in a motor rewind, and/or replacement of bearings, but not a rotor repair. When the motor returns to service, the same problem remains but with new insulation and/or bearings to destroy.

One method of testing the rotor condition <u>off-line</u> and with the motor installed in its circuit is the Rotor Influence Check (RIC™). RIC is a test performed on AC induction, synchronous, and wound rotor motor stators and is used to evaluate the magnetic coupling between the rotor and stator. This relationship indicates the condition of the rotor (and air gap discussed under Fault Zone 6 below) within the motor. Results correlate with but are more definitive than on-line testing using current signature analysis, as described in more detail in Chapters 9 and 12 (Volume 3).

The Rotor Influence Check is performed by rotating the rotor in specific increments (determined by the number of poles) over a single pole group, and recording inductance measurements for each phase of the 3 phase motor. For proper resolution, 18 inductance measurements per pole group are recommended. To determine the number of poles in a motor use the following equation.

$F = NP / 120$

F = Line Frequency (normally 60hz in North America)

N = Speed of the motor in RPM

P = # of poles

Recalculated: $P = 7200 / RPM$

Example:

A motor with name plate RPM = 1780 would have how many poles?

$P = 7200 / 1780$

= 4 poles

A RIC must be performed to provide up-to-date information about rotor condition. Faults such as broken rotor bars, cracked end rings or damaged laminations can exist even if the balance of inductance is low (good). If you are basing the decision to perform a RIC only on how high the balance of inductance is on a periodic or baseline motor circuit analysis test, you could be overlooking early-to-late stages of rotor cage defects. Figure 6-38 shows the expected inductance changes for a cage rotor with defects (which in this case turned out to be broken rotor bars).

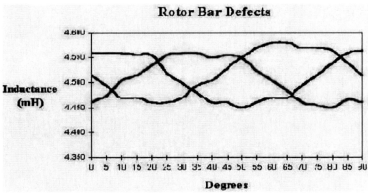

Figure 6-38 - RIC Test Showing Cage Rotor (Bar) Defects

Note the erratic inductance values at the peak of the sine waves for each phase. Broken rotor bars cause a skewing in the field flux generated by and around the rotor bars.

A normal rotor would have no skewing or erratic inductance patterns, as seen in Figure 6-39.

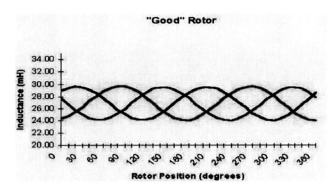

Figure 6-39 - RIC of Cage Rotor with No Defects

Fault Zone 6 – Air Gap – The air gap between AC rotor and stator or armature and stationary field of a DC motor is an important feature that can affect motor performance. If this air gap is not evenly sustained at all times as the rotating element turns 360 degrees, uneven magnetic fields can be produced. These magnetic imbalances can cause movement of windings, resulting in winding failure, and electrically induced vibration resulting in bearing failure. The faulty relationship between the rotor and stator or armature and stationary field is an eccentricity. The first type is called static eccentricity. Figure 6-40 shows an example of what static eccentricity looks like, physically and inductively.

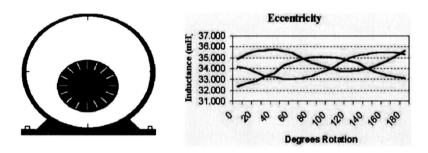

Figure 6-40 - Static Eccentricity

This type of eccentricity is caused by problems like a misaligned end bell or the shaft sitting low in the bearing. The physical result is that the shaft is always in the same place out of the electric center. The result is the variation or distortion in peaks of the sine waves created by inductive influence between rotor and stator across the air gap.

The second type of eccentricity is called dynamic eccentricity. This results when the rotor does not stay in one place but is allowed to move within the space of the stator as seen in Figure 6-41.

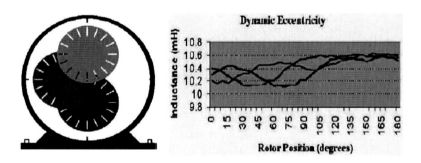

Figure 6-41- Dynamic Eccentricity

The inductive result is the movement of all three inductance values up or down, depending on which phase is closest to the rotor at a given degree rotation.

Conclusions Concerning Fault Zone Analysis - If at all possible, do not make a quick decision. If the decision is up to you as to what to do in a troubleshooting or diagnostic situation, look at the whole picture. Break the system down into its individual fault zones. Test each fault zone completely with every technology available to you, and finally make your recommendations written or verbal using the terminology used in fault zone analysis to express your confidence and capabilities.

[i]Figures in this chapter came from the following sources: Figures 6-1, EPRI Power Plant Electrical Reference Series Volume 16 Handbook to Assess the Insulation Condition of Large Rotating Machines G. Stone PhD et. al, authors; Figures 6-7, 6-8 & 6-9 EPRI Power Plant Electrical Reference Series Volume 6 Motors R.L. Nailen, P.E. author; Figures 6-10, 6-15 thru 6-18, 6-20, 6-21 & 6-22, courtesy of PdMA Corporation Noah Bethel; Figure 6-19 See note vii below; Figures 6-12, 6-13, 6-14 See note iv. below. Figures 6-2 thru 6-6, 6-11, 6-13, 6-23, 6-24 thru 6-28 & 6-29 -J. Nicholas. Figure 6-28 from Wikipedia Free Dictionary, modified by J. Nicholas. Remainder from Noah Bethel per footnote at the beginning of the section entitled "Indentifying Defects through Fault Zone Analysis" on page 43.

[ii]Case studies involving HiPot testing were provided from Baker Instrument Company (now an SKF subsidiary) from corporate marketing literature with permission given to use them from Curt Lanham, President.

[iii] Penrose, Howard W. PhD "A Review of Polarization Index and IEEE Standard 43-2000" available from EC& M website:

http://ecmweb.com/mag/electric_review_polarization_index/.

[iv] Case Study presented by Evan McCallum, Stewart & Stevenson Operations Inc, at PdMA Corporation Annual Conference May 15, 1996 in Tampa, FL.

[v] Ibid.

[vi] Case study and all figures provided by Noah Bethel Vice president PdMA Corporation, Tampa, FL and used with his permission.

[vii] Case Study and Figure by Don Shaw, Lead Electrician at Alcoa Davenport, IA during annual conference of PdMA Corporation, Tampa, FL. Mr. Shaw joined PdMA after retirement from Alcoa.

[viii] The NEMA Derating Curve is found in MG-1 1-14.35 A significant paper describing the origin and basis for the derating curve is: "Overheating Electric Motors: One Root Cause of Insulation Failure" available at
http://www.whitelegg.com/products/files/bcs_Overheating_Electric_Motors.pdf.

[ix] Improved Motors for Utility Applications EPRI EL-4286, Vol 1 & 2 Final Report, 1 October 1982.

CHAPTER 7

Core and Growler Testing[i]

Introduction - Any motor last rewound before the mid-1980's has a high probability of at least some core damage due to use of excessive heat to aid in old winding removal. That's because temperature control during "burnout" of old windings was not widely practiced before then. Prodded by many customers who wanted machines rewound and returned as soon as possible, repair shops used any means possible, including exposure to high temperatures in ovens (or worse -- use of handheld torches) to rapidly soften and burn out insulation materials from core slots so the old windings could be removed and new ones installed. Studies showed that core damage could result from excessive temperatures. When thin insulating coatings on laminations were destroyed, it effectively turned the laminated core into the equivalent of a solid core. This caused excessive heating due to eddy currents and hysteresis resulting in rapid deterioration of newly installed insulation systems when returned to operation.

Following advice from organizations such as Electrical Apparatus Service Association, shop owners (to protect themselves against failures within the post repair warranty period) and motor owners (to prevent unexpected failures in newly refurbished machines from interrupting production) began specifying and using burnout temperatures (discussed later) that didn't cause core lamination damage. More advanced repair shops began installing and using temperature monitoring and process recording devices such as that depicted in Figure 7-1. The loss of motor use because of longer repair time in the shop was easily made up by fewer lost production days due to premature failures.

Figure 7-1 - Burnout Oven Temperature Recorder

Burnout process control is also mentioned in Chapter 13 (Volume 4) as an item to check during repair shop audits. This chapter provides some details on performance of and reporting on core testing.

Cage damage, primarily in fabricated rotors, may be defined and localized by a number of different methods, some more difficult than others. One particularly graphic and easy to use method involves use of a "Growler" or half- transformer and simple tools, which will be described and illustrated in this chapter.

<u>Core, Core Loss or Loop Testing</u> - This test method was developed in late 1970's and early 1980's when it became obvious that motor core damage could be a root cause of overheating and failure of winding insulation systems and reduced motor efficiency. The test unit energizes the core to about 85,000 lines per square inch flux density using a low voltage, high current signal in a "loop" of cable passing through the core of a stator or pair of shaft clamps that pass current through a rotating assembly (rotor or armature) via its shaft.

As a starting point, core tester algorithms use "watts per pound" data provided by "electrical" steel manufacturers. Figure 7-2 shows a typical core test setup. The test unit is to the right of a large motor stator being examined. Two test leads, a (big) "loop" cable, to induce eddy currents and hysteresis in core laminations and a (small) voltage sensor cable pass through the core and return to the test unit. In the earliest days of conducting this test core "hot spots," created by eddy currents excited in the areas of laminations that had damage would be sensed by hand, as indicated in Figure 7-2.

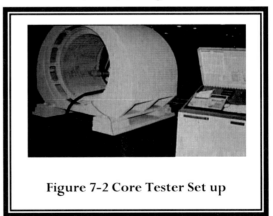

Figure 7-2 Core Tester Set up

As infrared thermography cameras became available they were employed to give a more definitive test result as depicted later in this chapter.

Core Test Computer – Dimensions (inches or centimeters) are inserted into the core test unit computer shown in Figure 7-3. It calculates the voltage needed to conduct the test based on algorithms or "curves" that have been developed from composite watts-per-pound data for a variety of most used "electrical" steel grades.

Figure 7-3 Core Test Computer and Operator Panel

Dimensions entered are:

- Core length
- Core diameter
- Back Iron depth
- Total slot depth
- Vent duct widths
- Number of vent ducts

For given core dimensions, the tester computer calculates <u>watts or kilowatts per pound</u> expected to be lost to eddy current generated heat, Ampere-Turns per inch and apparent Power Factor. Test result evaluation criteria will be discussed later in this chapter.

Core Tests of Rotors and Armatures – Core tests of rotor or armature laminations employ clamps (one on each end of the rotating element shaft) to direct current for energizing eddy currents and hysteresis excitation. Figure 7-4 shows a rotor with the loop cable connecting clamp installed on the shaft at the far end. The cable is attached using the Copper receptacle shown in the photo.

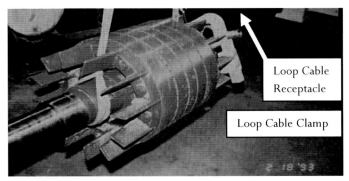

Figure 7-4 - Rotor with Core Test Loop Cable Clamp Installed (at Far End)

Figure 7-5 shows a rotor with cable clamps (loop cable attached) and sensor cable. The test unit is in the background.

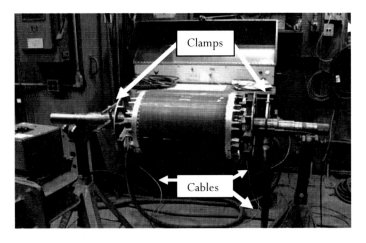

Figure 7-5 Rotor Rigged for Core Test

<u>Testing Core Laminations For Shorts</u> - This test is used on cores of stators, rotors and armatures. Low voltage with high current and frequency is used to induce eddy currents and hysteresis in a core. The type of steel used in core along with core manufacturing methods and conditions determines "rating" used to establish test conditions and evaluate results. Shorted or otherwise damaged laminations and core will cause larger eddy currents and hysteresis and higher losses. If losses are excessive, the shop may have to repair or scrap and replace a core.

Eddy Currents and Hysteresis – Figure 7-6 illustrates the effect of the high frequency magnetic field created by the alternating current passing through the "loop" cable circuit in a solid steel core and a core of the same outer dimensions and volume made up of three (3) thin sheets or laminations. Note that these are made of steel, a metal that will conduct currents. As discussed in Chapter 1 (Volume 1), the magnetic flux lines passing over the core components (creating relative motion) cause currents to be induced. The currents can't go anywhere, because the steel outer surfaces are insulated with a thin coating resistive to current flow between laminations or out of the core to supporting parts. So they "eddy" or circulate in the respective segments of the core, creating heat.

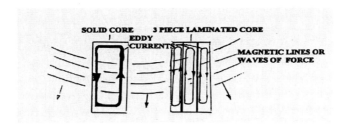

Figure 7-6 Eddy Currents Induced In Core Components

Reducing the thickness of the core laminations reduces power loss from eddy currents and hysteresis by a factor of the square of the number of laminations in the same volume. In this case the total of currents in the laminated core divided into 3 sheets is only one-ninth the current in the solid core of the same dimensions. Hysteresis loss results from energy used as molecules of iron are reversed by (alternating) current flowing in a motor. Both eddy currents and hysteresis produce heat, which is a threat to insulation and structural integrity of motor components.

Core Design Factors Affecting Losses - Core losses are affected by the following factors:

- Lamination thickness – **Most important factor**
- Lamination punching or stamping burrs
- Lamination clamping pressure (to hold the laminations together inside the frame)
- Type of insulation coating used on steel
- Heat treatment process used on punched laminations (Annealing can greatly reduce eddy   current and hysteresis loss in individual laminations)
- Lamination assembly method
- Silicon content and hardness of steel

Core Test Performance Criteria - The computer will indicate for the core dimensions the level of voltage needed for the test and the number of amps that <u>should be</u> observed at that level. Then voltage is increased to the level specified and the actual amps flowing is compared to the calculated estimate. A basic test evaluation comes down to two criteria:

If lower than amps estimate → good core

If higher than amps estimate → some core damage

Core Testing Laminations for Shorts - As a final step in the core test procedure, the level of current is raised to two or three times the normal test amps for about one minute (longer for larger cores). Then, using either a human hand or (more effectively) as illustrated in Figure 7-7, an infrared thermography image, hot spots (>10°C over surrounding area) are located and marked (e.g. with chalk) for correction. Hotspots are easily documented

Figure 7-7 Core Loss Test Showing Hot Spot

and rechecked for proof of repair success by recording before and after infrared images.

Core Condition Evaluation[ii] - A core loss algorithm is used to calculate Watts per pound (Watts/#) . This is the most important item in a core loss evaluation.

The actual values measured are compared to "Good" "Marginal" and "Bad" criteria below:

> 2-5 Watts/# =>Good
>
> 6-8 Watts/# =>Marginal
>
> > 8 Watts/# =>Bad

(Range runs 0 to 10 Watts/#)

Apparent Power Factor - Watts/Reactive Current x Voltage = Watts/VARS - Range 0.2 to 0.9; (indicates relative amount of reactive power needed to produce the magnetic flux used in the test compared to the actual power lost (Watts) to eddy currents

> Lower → Good
>
> Higher → Bad

Ampere-Turns per inch (AT/IN) — Range is 0 to 26 AT/IN - Lower is better.

Computer compares AT/IN to an empirically derived composite of published curves of AT/IN versus Flux Density used for evaluation over many years for core testing and found to be accurate for greater than 90% of new and old cores tested.

The computer then indicates imposed flux in lines per inch.

Typical Report of Core Condition - Besides date of test and job number, dimensional input data used in the computer (as indicated above) is reported (and must match actual unit tested).

In addition the report will contain:

Computed estimated comparison data: Volts; Approximate Amps; Approximate Watts

Measured data: Actual Volts, Amps, Watts and Power Factor

Results and Recommendations:

- For all conditions (Good, Marginal and Bad) the report should give: Measured Watts per pound, AT/IN, AT/IN from experience curves (along with maximum value in range of each) and Flux Density as discussed above
- Example for bad core: Core loss too high! Take corrective steps and retest or reject and re-core or replace motor.

In most cases for motors below 50-100 Horsepower, replacing the whole motor is more economical than re-coring. Replacing core laminations is a solution generally practiced for motors not normally stocked because of special features or designs requiring long lead time to replicate.

Relative Comparison of Core Loss Data - Because of the nature of the measurement and calculation of core loss and the assumptions and generalization of multiple source data into a set of "curves," the best method for evaluating core loss is to compare core loss data when the motor is new (if you can get it conveniently) to core loss when the motor is received in the shop for repair. Core loss should be the same with and without the winding installed. Compare core loss from before the removal of the winding, if replacement is contemplated, to that from after removal using any heating or mechanical method or combination thereof.

Any increase in core loss implies the probability that motor will not be as efficient when placed back into service.

Core Hotspot Correction -- There are a variety of tools and insulating materials used to eliminate hotspots. These include but are not limited to:

- Plastic or hard rubber hammers (to pound on core ends to "crack" it, which sometimes causes hotspots to disappear)

- Hammer and sharpened hack saw blade (to separate laminations welded at the surface usually by a rotor strike in service or by improper removal in the shop)

- Insulating spray (that may be applied between separated laminations)

- Grinders to remove surfaces of laminations that have been "peened over" due to a rotor strike (or it may happen during motor disassembly).

Using a sharpened hacksaw blade to separate core laminations, as shown in Figure 7-8, is most effective most of the time in eliminating small area hotspots in motor cores.

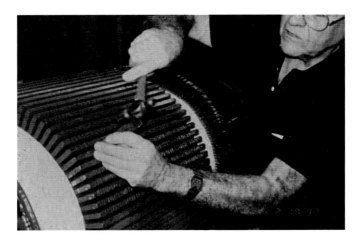

Figure 7-8 - Core Hotspot Correction

In the worst case, when a replacement isn't immediately available, a motor must be re-cored either with new or refurbished laminations. This is not uncommon for older, large motors.

Figure 7-9 shows a failed rotor core being removed because laminations were too badly damaged to repair.

Figure 7-9 - Damaged Rotor Core Being Removed

Core Test Case Study – A Commonwealth Aluminum Rolling Mill drive motor armature winding failed to ground during full load operation as shown in Figure 7-10. A spare was available and was installed. Root cause of failure was found to be poor quality control of last armature rewind 5 years earlier. Close up of major damage in Figure 7-11 shows laminations, apparently intact. Question of whether inter-laminar insulation was damaged was resolved favorably by a core test prior to full rewind of the armature.

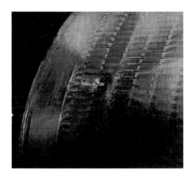

Figure 7-10 - Rolling Mill Drive Motor Armature

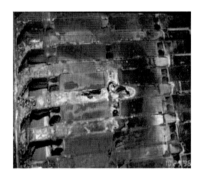

Figure 7-11 - Close up of Armature Damage

Avoiding Increased Core Loss and Decreased Efficiency - Ensure that when ordering motor winding replacement that old winding removal is done under closely controlled conditions.

Limit "burn-out" oven temperature

680°F (360°C) for laminations with organic coating

750°F (400°C) for laminations with inorganic coating

Lower temperatures don't always soften insulation materials sufficiently to "clean" the core when conductors are finally removed. Ensure mechanical tools used to remove old winding coils and remaining insulation do not damage core laminations, either.

Alternative Core Test Method[iii] - Portable devices can be taken into the field for core testing small sections of a large motor core. An excitation loop is energized through the core with rotor removed. The core tester sensor (Chottock Potentiometer Coil) is positioned across a section of the core to detect the magnetic field of the eddy currents induced by the excitation loop.

Figure 7-12 shows the Iris Power Engineering EL CID unit in use for generator and motor cores. An excitation loop excites eddy currents in the core.

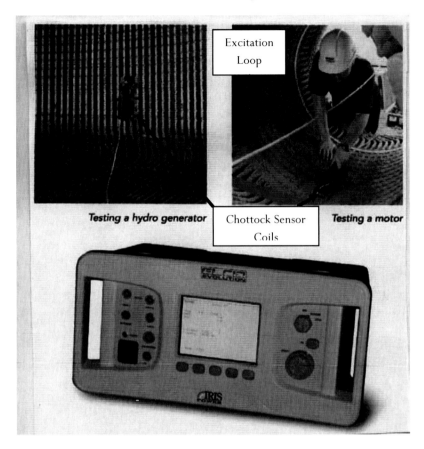

Excitation Loop

Testing a hydro generator

Chottock Sensor Coils

Testing a motor

Figure 7-12 – EL CID Portable Core Tester in use for Motor and Generator Core

Core Energizing Loop - Core is energized to produce eddy currents in manner similar to other core or loop tests. As shown in Figure 7-13, a low voltage AC power source cable is looped through the core center to excite eddy currents.

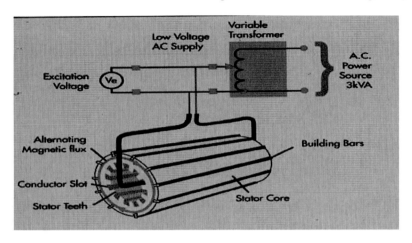

Figure 7-13 Excitation Loop

<u>Motor Core Tester Sensor</u> – A Chottock Potentiometer symbolized in Figure 7-14 is used to sense magnetic fields produced by eddy currents induced to flow in the core. Reading is interpreted to indicate presence of larger-than-normal (fault) eddy currents caused by damaged laminations.

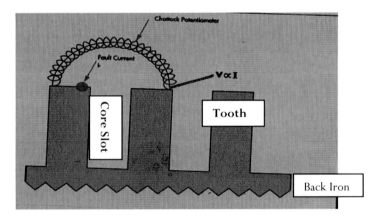

Figure 7-14 – Chottock Potentiometer Sensor Coil Detects Larger than Normal (Fault) Eddy Currents Indicating Core Damage

The voltage variation is proportional to the size of the fault eddy current and its magnetic field.

Motor Core Test Signals - Sensor is capable of sensing with flux excitation levels of about 4 percent of that seen in service. Figure 7-15 shows how test results appear on tester screen.

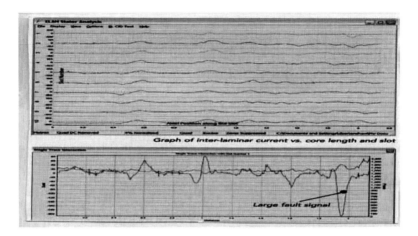

Figure 7-15 - Motor Core Test Signals

Another screen allows a view of conditions of the entire core using a "map" showing good areas of the core in green, marginal areas in yellow and areas needing attention in red.

Tests for Cage Damage [iv]- ADWEL International Ltd (acquired by Iris Power Engineering in 2007) for many years sold a unit called the Motor Core Tester. It operates on principles (Chottock Potentiometer Sensing) similar to the one described above. Many of these units are still in use. Figure 7-16 illustrates results of testing a 46 bar Squirrel Cage Rotor. The image shows damage to at least four bars.

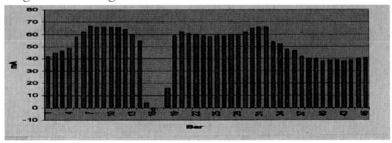

Figure 7-16 - Testing for Cage Damage on 46 Bar Rotor with Core Tester

Growlers - Growlers are basically constructed by wrapping a coil of wire around a laminated iron core, making it like the "primary" half of a transformer. Many are "homemade" but commercial versions are available. They come in various sizes from hand held to bench mounted or separately mounted on a rolling frame. Growlers are typically energized with single phase 115-120 Volt 60 Hz or 220-240 Volt 50 Hz power. They are found in every motor repair shop.

They are used to energize conductors of motor components by "transformer action" in conjunction with a thin steel strip (like a hack saw blade) to reveal shorts or opens in cage rotors, wave wound armatures and induction motor stators.

Growler Testing – This test induces current flow by transformer action if a circuit to ground is present. Location is found using hack saw blade, metal ruler or thin steel strip which vibrates or "growls," giving rise to the test name. Sparks caused by passing the steel sensor strip touching on adjacent commutator bars indicates shorts in coils connected to these bars. (Works for Wave Wound, <u>not</u> Lap Wound with cross connected (equalized) coils.) Figure 7-17 shows a growler test of an armature.

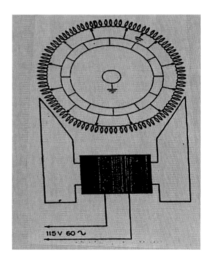

Figure 7-17 Growler Test of Armature

Growler and Magnetic Sheet Testing - Growler and magnetic sheet testing is used to find defective rotor bars. The magnetic sheet is really two sheets of translucent plastic sealed at the edges to contain a thin oil carrying iron particles suspended in it. The sheet is laid on the surface of a cage rotor as it rests on a growler (or vice-versa), and the growler is energized. Bars that are functioning as designed will conduct currents, which in turn create magnetic fields that cause the iron particles to concentrate and align over the "good" bars. Open (cracked or disconnected) bars will <u>not</u> conduct current (thus no magnetic field) and will not show alignment of particles in the sheet above the affected bar. Figures 7-18 & 7-19 illustrate this method of testing for rotor bar damage.

Figure 7-18 – Growler and Magnet Sheet Test for Rotor Breaks

Figure 7-19 - Growler and Magnetic Sheet Test of Large rotor

<u>**Growler Testing Large Squirrel Cage Rotor**</u> – The growler in Figure 7-19 is the object on top of the rotor which is inducing current to flow in the cage, aligning particles in the magnetic sheets nearest "good" bars.

<u>**Growler Testing Stator Winding for Shorts**</u> - Growlers may also be used to test a stator winding for shorts to ground. With rotor removed, place a growler on bottom of stator interior and energize it to cause

"transformer action" in the winding. Move the growler around the circumference of the stator, slot to slot. Place a hack saw blade or thin steel strip close to the core aligned to the axis of the rotor on the other side of the coil being energized. The blade will vibrate if a short is located in a particular coil. This is seldom done unless one uses a light-weight hand held growler with enough energy to work (available from commercial vendors).

---

[i] Sources of figures in this chapter are: Figures 7-1 thru 7-4, 7-6, 7-8 thru 7-10, 7-18 and 7-19 - J. Nicholas; Figures 7-5 and 7-7 G. Generalovic; Figures 7-12 thru 7-16 Iris Power Engineering (See endnote iii below); Figure 7-17 (modified by J. Nicholas) source unknown, but believed in the public domain.

[ii] Criteria may vary depending upon the OEM of the core test unit. Some have proprietary methods and report results accordingly and may not compare with results from core test units from competitors. The information on evaluation is somewhat of a composite from different core tester OEM literature, but relies mostly on LEXSECO, LLC, Louisville, KY information. An excellent article on core testing entitled "Core Loss Testing in the Practical Motor Repair Environment" is available from http://www.lexseco.com/files/Lexseco_WhitePaper.pdf.

[iii] Material on alternative core testing including images (modified to add explanatory notes) is from a combination of a paper on core testing using the ADWEL Motor Core Tester (MCT) unit by David Bertenshaw, July 2000 posted on the website of ADWEL International Ltd. (since merged into Iris Power Engineering - Iris) and the Iris EL CID product brochure. Iris dropped the MCT from its product line, concentrating instead on the EL CID Evolution[TM] unit. Dr. Greg Stone, Ph.D., VP of Iris, gave permission to use information on EL CID and from Bertenshaw's paper in this text on 15 September 2010. EL CID stands for "Electromagnetic Core Imperfection Detection." The first EL CID units were developed by Central Electricity Generating Board facility staff in the United Kingdom. The test technique involving use of the Chottock Potentiometer in various forms is used world-wide for core testing."

[iv] One of the best recent papers on rotor cage testing written by Tom Bishop, Technical Support Specialist at EASA and entitled "Squirrel Cage Rotor Testing" was presented at the EASA Convention in San Francisco, CA 30 June 2003 and is available for viewing or download at http://www.pumpingmachinery.com/pumpmagazine/pumparticles/article_29/rotortesting.pdf.

APPENDIX C

PowerPoint® Slides for Volume 2

Chapter 5

**Surge and Surge Comparison
Testing of Motors**

Chapter 5

of

Motor Electrical Predictive
Maintenance & Testing

1

Surge Testing

- Been in use for over 80 years

- Earlier test, similar in nature, called "Rylander Test" developed and patented in mid-1920's

- To limit current during the test a high frequency "pulsing" (15-200KHz) or oscillating voltage is used, making use of characteristic high "reactance" of coils

- Test Voltage is determined by rated line voltage for the motor or coil being tested (plus an additional amount to establish a "margin" to offset effects of aging over time)

2

Surge Testing of Motors

- Insertion of high energy (low current) DC Voltage pulses with fast rise times (decaying transient) into motor electrical coils
  - AC stator or wound rotor phase coils,
  - DC motor armature and field coils,
  - Synchronous rotor pole coils
- Combination of the tester and the coil(s) under test form an electrical circuit with its own characteristics
- Pulses between coil winding and test set and are affected (dampened) by impedance encountered
- Wave form analysis or "ringing" frequency analysis used to detect problems such as grounds, shorts, opens or reversed coils

3

Surge Testing of Motors

- A single coil or winding made up of several coils is examined at increasing voltage levels while looking for indication of a fault such as:
  - Turn-to-turn insulation damage
  - Short to ground
  - Improperly connected (reversed) coil(s)
- Test wave form of inserted wave is observed on an oscilloscope
  - Shape and stability of the waveform are used to determine condition

4

Surge Testing of Motors

- Electrical coils have very low resistance (which can be ignored in what follows) and a large Inductance (Symbol L for Inductance)

- Inductance is the property of an electric circuit where a change in an electric current through it induced an electromotive force (voltage) that opposes the change in current.

- A surge tester generates a pulse for insertion into a coils by "charging" a capacitor or electronic equivalent circuit (Symbol C for capacitance) with electrons

5

Surge Test Principles

- **The combination of tester and coil or winding under test:**
  - Forms what is called a "Bell Circuit," in electrical terms, where the pulse "ringing frequency" between the Capacitor in the tester and the coil in the motor can be determined

  - Frequency of the "ringing" is determined by the formula "1 divided by $2\pi LC$"

  - If "L" of the coil changes because of a fault (e.g., short) the frequency of the circuit between coil and tester changes

6

Surge Testing of Motors

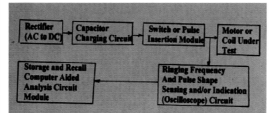

Simplified block diagram of a modern computer aided surge tester connected to a motor or motor coil for analysis

7

Surge Testing of Motors

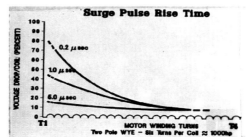

Surge pulse distributes across coils being tested so peak (and force is greater in the coils nearest the tester connection point

8

Surge Testing

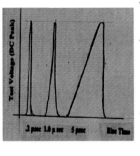

- Pulses with shorter rise-times penetrate deeper into the winding coils
- Pulses "stress-test" the insulation around the turns of a winding coil, without hurting them because current flow with short pulses is quite low
- Points where the insulation has deteriorated will be revealed when arcing occurs, simulating what happens in actual service

9

Surge Testing

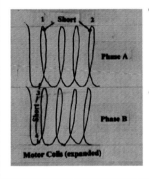

- Short between points 1 & 2 –Turn-to-turn - deprives all turns between the two points of current =>no magnetic field from that part of coil that is "shorted"
- Short between points 3 & 4 – Phase-to-phase - diverts current and changes strength and shape of magnetic field from affected coils

10

Surge & Surge Comparison Testing

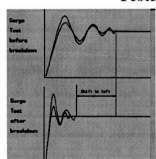

- One of few tests that can detect turn-to-turn or phase-to-phase shorts in motors
- Shorted coils dampen inserted wave pulse, have a higher resonant frequency and instability due to arcs
- Relationship given by formula "1 divided by 2☆LC," where the "C" is provided by the tester (a constant) and "L" is provided by the winding (varies depending on condition)

11

Surge Testing of Motors

- When Voltage <u>difference</u> between adjacent conductors of coil(s) rises to a certain level (defined by a relationship called Paschen's Law), arcing will occur through damaged insulation

    - Paschen's law also requires a minimum 335 volts for test at atmospheric pressure

- The arcing occurs at the point of a "short" where current <u>bypasses some number of turns</u> <u>in the same coil</u> or <u>flows between turns in separate coils</u>

- The arcing caused by the current flowing between turns is typically intermittent as repeated "pulses" are injected into the winding being tested   12
    - Resulting wave form appears "collapsed and unstable"

Surge Testing of Motors

- When the surge test pulses cause arcing between turns of a coil or motor, the overall impedance of the circuit changes
    - The biggest change is in the inductance (capacitance of the tester is constant – resistance of the circuit changes just a little bit and can be ignored)
    - The ringing frequency of the circuit made up of the motor and tester changes (increases)
    - On an oscilloscope, the effect is to shift the wave form to the left (closer to its origin on the screen)
    - On an undamped oscilloscope, the arcing creates the appearance of "flickering" "jitter" or instability   13

Surge Comparison Testing

- Comparison is made between two or more "bell frequency" wave forms from motor coils or phases of a motor
    - Phases of a multi-phase motor should have exactly the same electrical characteristics (and wave forms) if perfect
    - If the wave forms are superimposed on a "multi-trace" oscilloscope they should overlap and appear as one trace
    - If one phase differs from either of the other two, there will be a difference in impedance (mostly caused by inductance) and the wave forms will not overlap   14

Surge Comparison Testing

- Comparisons in three phase motors are made two at a time - Phases 1 to 2, 2 to 3 and 3 to 1.
  - Fault will be revealed by mismatched trace of the phase containing the fault compared to the 2 "good" phases
- When tested coil or winding surge pulse characteristics are "compared" either to a "master" or to each other in a given unit or situation, "Surge Comparison" is occurring
- If no master is available, revert to a straight "surge test" raising test voltage in steps to recommended limit or until wave form collapse or instability occurs: then remove voltage immediately to preserve whatever life of the insulation is left and to prevent collateral damage

15

Surge Comparison Testing

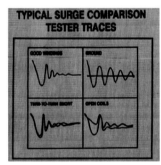

- Analysis is performed on a multi-trace oscilloscope
- Wave forms may be stored for future comparison
- Valuable test during initial construction, rewind and when intermittent problems develop
- Also used during motor insulation system diagnostic & rewind
- Predictive analysis also possible

16

Surge and Surge Comparison Testing

- Analysts skilled in surge testing become familiar with oscilloscope wave forms and can tell from their characteristic shapes or "traces" the types of defects most likely present
- Faults in single phase and DC motor components are revealed when mismatch occurs between the coil under test and a "master" known to be representative of a good winding or coil
- Modern surge testers have the capability of storing "known" wave forms and automatically comparing them to those from a tested unit, supporting conclusions using "pattern recognition" analysis

17

Determination of Surge Test Voltage

- All insulation can be caused to fail at some level of voltage applied
- To assure no risk to insulation when new and in-service, various authoritative sources of "standards" have established recommended levels for testing based on Line Voltage or expected (nameplate) Voltage rating at motors
- Sources include:
  - IEEE 95- Insulation Testing and IEEE 522- Surge Testing
  - Electrical Apparatus Service Association – EASA
  - IEC 34-15   18

Surge & Surge Comparison Testing - Max Voltage - New & In-service

- All standards recommend testing voltage be lowered (from value when new) for in-service Surge Testing and for testing coils before cured with insulating materials

- EASA, NEMA & IEC recommend 65% of test voltage when new

- IEEE 522 Recommends 75% of test voltage when new

19

Surge Test Maximum Voltage

- In general, for all DC test voltages for motors (480 to 13,800 Volts AC) the formula 2E + 1000 Volts (E=Line Volts in DC units – 1 for 1 AC to DC) gives a value that is:

  - Aggressively high to slightly lower for low voltage motors

  - Conservative to very conservative for high voltage motors

  20

SURGE (& HI POT) TESTING VOLTAGES

- **Per NEMA MG-1**

  –Section 12.13– Apply 1000 + 2 X Rated Volts to New Windings
  –Section 3.01 – Apply 75% of Voltage for in Service testing
  –Section 20.48 – DC Voltage test = 1.7 X AC Voltage
  Example for 460 Volt AC Motor Using DC Tester

          1000 + 2 x 460 Volts = 1920 Volts (AC) -New
                                  x .75 In-service
                                  1440 Volts (AC)
     "Energy difference factor" x 1.7 AC to DC
                                  2448 Volts DC

- **2448 Volts DC is conservative compared to IEC standard, aggressive compared to IEEE 95 & 522.**

21

SURGE & HI POT TESTING VOLTAGES

- **Per ANSI & IEEE Standard 95/2002**

  Section 5.1 DC test voltage = 1.7 x AC test voltage
  Section 5.2 - maintenance proof testing should be between 125-150% of rated volts

  Example for 4160 Volt (AC) motor:

  2 x 4160 + 1000 Volts = 9320 Volts DC

4160	4160	
x 1.25	x 1.5	
5200	6240	
x 1.7	x 1.7	AC to DC "energy" factor
8840	10,600 Volts (DC)	

  - 9320 Volts is between 125 & 150% recommended by IEEE 95

22

Surge Testing Considerations

- **Point of connection will affect test results**
  - Results for connection at MCC will differ from test connection at motor disconnected from a circuit
    - ✓ Connecting cables have all three factors of impedance present, also

- **Rotor "coupling" or "rotor loading" will affect traces on display of tester, causing more rapid dampening and must be "cancelled" by positioning rotor or accounted for if movement isn't possible**

- **Traces from large AC motors with parallel connected winding coils are harder to interpret because of little or no trace separation (Inductance change is small relative to overall impedance of the winding)**

23

Surge Testing Considerations

- Traces from motors with a large number of coils in series are also hard to interpret

- Small separations of "traces" on an oscilloscope are normal and generally no cause for alarm

- In Wound Rotor and Synchronous machines lifting brushes and shorting slip rings is needed to cancel coupling effect

24

Surge Comparison Testing Considerations (Continued)

- In AC & DC machines with multiple windings all but the winding under test should be grounded to eliminate inductive coupling effects
  - Equalized windings may affect wave traces but are ok if a "rhythmic shift" is observed as armature rotated

- Surge capacitors and capacitors for power factor correction must be disconnected from the motor circuit under test to avoid overloading the tester and suppressing the presence of faults
  - Trace comparisons aren't as obvious   25

Surge Comparison Testing Considerations (Continued)

- When testing wound rotors and synchronous motor rotor field poles while installed, stator windings must be shorted and brushes lifted to prevent coupling effect and diode damage
- All windings and magnetic material close to coils under test must be the same for all so that valid comparison must be made
  - For example, test all DC motor field poles of a motor while installed or all while on a bench alone
  - Coils differ in inductance due to different permeability between iron and air

26

Surge Comparison Test Considerations

- With the same number of coils and turns in each phase, Wye and Delta connected 3 phase motors will have different wave forms on the analysis oscilloscope
- Because "basket" or concentric wound motors have different lengths of magnet wire in the coils, there will be some small amount of separation between traces from each phase
  - As long as they are close in shape and very stable, there's nothing to be alarmed about
  - Same holds true for shunt coils in DC motors

27

Surge Comparison Test Considerations

- When testing "chiller" or hermetically sealed motors, consultation with manufacturer's instructions is prudent
  - May have to bring internal pressure to near atmospheric to avoid damage to the winding under test

- Surge test is usually done second in sequence with Hi Pot test
  - Use Hi Pot test result as the upper limit for maximum voltage to apply during surge testing

- May also be used with special test procedures on:
  - Transformers
  - Coil Heaters

28

Surge Test Risks to Motor Condition

- Users and vendors have raised an issue of risk when using high voltage for testing

- Over time, this has become a non-issue, based on experience of no documented claims to the contrary and no legal claims for liability from users or owners upon surge test equipment vendors

29

Surge Test Risks to Motor Condition

- Numerous users have employed this method for in service over decades of years without apparent harm to motors tested

- Consensus is that if the motor insulation is weak, it is far better to find the emerging problem during the test (which must be done while shut down) than in normal operation when other losses may occur

30

Surge Test Risks to Motor Condition

- Surge test with its insertion of multiple high voltage pulses at high frequency (and low current) over a period of a few minutes of testing each year:
  - Doesn't raise temperature of motor during test
  - Is far less a threat than over-voltage pulses from VFD's or from inductive load starts and stops that induce random and repeated voltage "spikes" on the supply busses many times each day
  - Has been proven in shop tests not to cause failure even when continued for <u>days</u> at a time at recommended maximum voltage level

31

Surge Test Risks to Motor Condition

- With its unique ability to find emerging turn-to-turn and phase-to-phase failures the relatively low risk of inducing a failure is more than offset by the benefit of avoiding failure during production
  - The unique feature of the surge test is its ability to find emerging winding failures at voltage levels well above alternative low voltage test methods (e.g., motor circuit analysis), providing added early warning, if needed
  - When a failure does occur during production, surge testing can quickly reveal the cause, leading to an early decision on the type of repair needed

32

Advanced Winding Surge & HiPot Tester

Computerized, capable of storage and comparison of wave forms and readings over time for multiple machines

33

Surge Comparison Test Case Study #1

- St. Johns River Power Park, Jacksonville, FL - 6900 Volt, 3 Phase, 600HP coal pulverizer motor tripped off line during lightning storm
- Check for grounds with resistance-to-ground (RTG) meter at 1000 & 5000 Volts showed no faults to ground, with readings acceptable
- Motor restart attempted, but it tripped again
- Motor set to shop where new Class H insulation systems and re-powering (from 500 to 600HP) rewind had been done 22 months before.
- Surge test showed insulation was breaking down at ~ 4600Volts
  - Pulsed DC simulates AC without high current   34
- RCFA determined lightning strike resulted in failure

Pulverizer Motor Winding Failure

Note the separations of the end turns in the area in the upper right. These are opposite the area of he connections in the same lead coils of the stator winding..

35

Surge Comparison Test Case Study #2

- Utility 4160 Volt 3 Phase pump motor circuit breaker tripped
- Resistance-to-ground reading was good
- Conductor path resistance also showed no problem
- Surge tester showed turn-to-turn fault at 500 Volts
  - Insulation breakdown was not complete until surge test stressed the winding to the point where the fault was revealed

36

Surge Comparison Test Case Study #3

- Chemical plant began initial surge testing of critical motors during plant shutdown immediately after receipt of their first tester
- 4160 Volt "stirring" motor inside a reactor vessel showed a turn-to-turn fault at 2000 Volts
- Failure when motor was in service would have required 12 hours just to get inside the vessel, and the batch in process would have been ruined
- Savings in this case exceeded cost of the tester

37

Surge Comparison Test Case Study #4

- Champion Paper Company 460 Volt, 3 Phase, 60 HP motor pulled for new bearings and other minor repairs
  - RTG showed "infinite"
  - Hi Pot to 2800 Volts DC satisfactory
  - Surge test showed phase-to-phase fault at 650 Volts
- Recommendation was to rewind because estimate was that it would only survive 2 or 3 more starts before failure
- Because motor had run ok before removal, it was placed back into service without further repair
- Motor failed during second start sequence after being reinstalled, shorted phase-to-phase

38

Chapter 6

High Potential (Hi Pot)
Resistance-to-Ground (RTG)
Polarization Index Profiles (PIPs)
and Diagnostic Tests

Chapter 6

Of

Motor Electrical Predictive
Maintenance & Testing

1

Introduction

- Insulation systems with all their various components and subsystems are vulnerable to many different failure mechanisms and causes
- Field testing done with instruments that use voltage consistent with rated values
- Motor manufacturers and rebuilders have more powerful testers to stress insulation systems with higher voltage levels
- Modern electronics and computers have been employed to provide more sophisticated ways of evaluating insulation system integrity

2

Insulation Systems

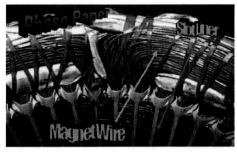

Complex with many components and "leak" paths

3

HIGH POTENTIAL TESTING

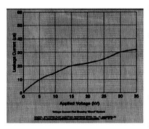

- Shop test moved by some to the field
- Winding isolated, frame grounded, potential transformers & thermal sensors shorted or grounded
- Use ramp or step Method
- Test takes 1-5 minutes

4

HIGH POTENTIAL (HI POT) TESTING

- **Industry acceptance test to assure insulation integrity**

- **Simple, easy application of force**

- **Ideal for new & rewound motors**

- **Test against a limit**

5

HIGH POTENTIAL TESTING

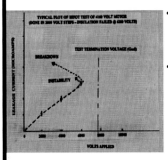

- **Typical AC insulation system should be able to withstand at least 1.5 times rated power**
- **DC systems often tested by "2, 3, 4, 5" Rule**
  - **2300/4000/6900 = 2E**
  - **460 = 3E**
  - **230 = 4E**
  - **110 = 5E**

6

TESTING DURING REWIND

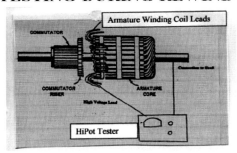

Hi Pot to see if coils damaged during insertion into slots 7
Done for all AC & DC motor components at various stages of the rewind process

Hi Pot Test Unit

Older Hi-Pot Tester has two controls & meters, one for voltage and the other for current 8

Computerized Hi Pot Test

Main readings are applied voltage and leakage current [9]

HIGH POTENTIAL TESTING

- Some fear test is destructive
  - EPRI Literature of 1980's tends to confirm this view
- Experts now view test as no threat to healthy insulation systems compared to threats from:
  - Voltage spikes or surges seen daily on grid and from nearby busses and facilities
  - VFDs that aren't working properly
  - Natural events (such as lightning) that occur frequently in some areas

10

HIGH POTENTIAL TESTING

- DC Voltage rather than AC is recommended (by EPRI)
  - DC gives earlier warning of instability

  - AC Voltage can cause breakdown with very little warning, through this is not always true

  - Above 2300 Volts (@ 1 atmosphere pressure) AC can cause corona discharge and rapid damage to insulation materials

11

Hi Pot Case Study #1

- Union Pacific Railroad tests all of the fleet's traction (DC) motors
- A 750HP 30 year old motor was tested and a coil breakdown was detected during a routine test
- Had the failure occurred in service the loss would have exceeded $100,000 because of delays

12

Hi Pot Case Study # 2

- Ameren Central Illinois Public Service electric utility conducts routine testing of all critical motors on a regular basis

- A 4160 Volt 3 Phase Motor was found to have a breakdown at a voltage level well below the maximum recommended for testing, $2E + 1000 = 9320$ Volts

- Investigation revealed close proximity of a phase connection with severely damaged insulation to the cover of terminal box

- Had motor failed plant was limited to 50% for a day and estimated replacement power cost was $643,288 per day

13

Hi Pot Case Study # 2

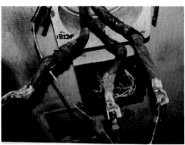

14

- Typical utility motor phase connection leads similar to the ones found with deteriorated insulation by Hi Pot test to be in danger of grounding to terminal box cap

INSULATION RESISTANCE-TO-GROUND TESTING

- Traditional method uses simple, inexpensive test units with DC voltage output
- Resistance relative to ground (nominal)
- Gives overall indication of insulation condition (up to a point)
- Current "leaks" to ground via multiple paths with one usually dominant when a motor is "grounded"

15

IEEE Std. 43-2000

Guidelines for dc voltages to be applied during insulation resistance test

Winding rated voltage (V)[a]	Insulation resistance test direct voltage
<1000	500
1000 – 2500	500 – 1000
2501 – 5000	1000 – 2500
5001 – 12,000	2500 – 5000
>12,000	5000 – 10,000

16

[a] Rated line-to-line voltage for 3 phase ac machines, line-to-ground voltage for 1-phase machines, and rated direct voltage for dc machines or field windings.

IEEE Std. 43-2000

Recommended minimum insulation resistance @ 40 degrees Celsius (all values in Megaohms)

Minimum insulation resistance	Test specimen
$IR_{1min} = kV + 1$	For most windings made before about 1970. All field windings, and others not described below
$IR_{1min} = 100$	For most DC armature and AC windings built after about 1970 (form-wound) coils
$IR_{1min} = 5$	For most machines with random-wound stator coils and form-wound coils rated below 1 kv. 17

Resistance to Ground & Current Flows

- **Three or four things occur when DC Voltage is impressed on a motor winding insulation**
  - **Capacitive charging current flows until the motor has reached its "capacity" to store electrons**
  - **Absorption current flows, but falls to zero in 1-2 minutes**
    - **Due to insulation molecules being polarized by electrons and**
    - **Drift current through molecular structure of insulation materials**
  - **Conduction Current may flow, but is essentially zero unless moisture has saturated the materials**
    - **Older insulation systems have natural higher conduction current**
  - **Leakage current flows through multiple conductive paths**
    - **This current is what remains after all of the currents above stabilize and forms the basis for Ohm's Law - I=E/R.**
    - **RTG meter measures Voltage & Current and indicates resistance-to-ground**

18

PERIODIC RTG READINGS

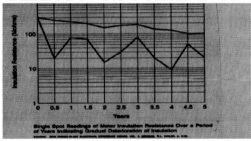

Single Spot Readings of Motor Insulation Resistance Over a Period of Years Indicating Gradual Deterioration of Insulation

- **Temperature & humidity affect readings**
- **Lower curve = Raw data**   19
- **Upper curve is "normalized" to a common value (typically 25 or 40°C) but never "normalized" for humidity and trend analyzed**

RTG and Polarization Index Curves

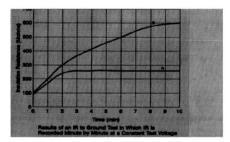

Results of an IR to Ground Test in Which IR is Recorded Minute by Minute at a Constant Test Voltage

- **Stable PI curves with data recorded every minute**

20

RATIOS OF RESISTANCE TO GROUND

- May be of some value, but often are misleading
- New IEEE 43 says to ignore if RTG>5000 Meg Ohms
- Apply to motors of all sizes
- For best application requires tester with upper range ~ 15 Gig Ohms or higher

21

RATIOS OF RESISTANCE TO GROUND

- 10 Minutes to 1 Minute
  Polarization Index Ratio
  >2 => Class F or Higher System OK
  <2 => System May Be Deteriorating
- 1 Minute to 30 Seconds:
  Dielectric Absorption Ratio
  ~ =>1.5 System OK
  < 1.25 => System May be Deteriorating

22

MEASURING LEAKAGE CURRENT

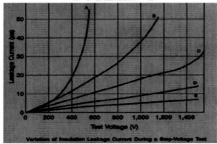

- Progressive Curves Taken As Motor Dries Out

23

INSULATION MATERIALS & TEMPERATURE

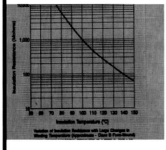

- Rule of thumb – for every 10° C increase RTG is halved
- Actual range is 8-14°
- Curves for classes F & H lie above and parallel to the one to the left

24

Impedance vs. Resistance-to-Ground

- Experts contend that RTG measured with DC voltage instruments provides only part of the assessment needed to understand true insulation system condition
- DC voltage tests may not detect voids in insulation systems of form wound stator coils caused by improper impregnation, thermal cycling and deterioration
- Impedance with three components – Resistance, Inductive reactance and Capacitive reactance (in particular) can. 25

Impedance Equation

X_C Sensitive to Voids

$$Z = \sqrt{R^2 + (X_L^2 - X_C^2)}$$

Where Inductive reactance $X_L = 2\pi f L$ and Capacitive reactive $X_C = \frac{1}{2\pi f C}$

f = frequency of the voltage imposed by the tester   If $f = 0$ X_L and $X_C = 0$ and $Z = R$

26

POLARIZATION INDEX
PROFILE - PIP

- Provides another indication of insulation system condition - stability
- Made possible by modern testers
- Plot of RTG vs Time with data taken every 3-5 seconds for 10 minutes
- Shows when system is beginning to show instability which will eventually result in low readings on any RTG instrument

27

Polarization Index Profile (PIP)

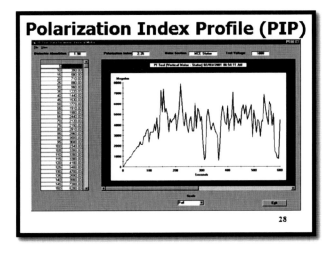

28

Stabilizing Insulation System Example: Fuel Oil Service Pump Motor PIP Case Study #1

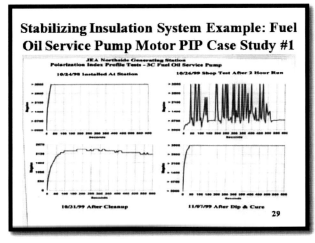

29

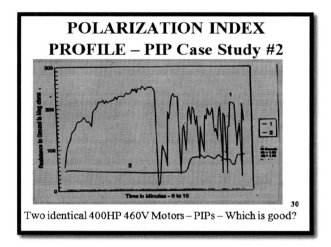

Two identical 400HP 460V Motors – PIPs – Which is good?

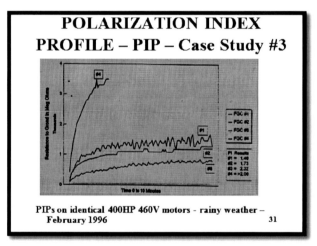

PIPs on identical 400HP 460V motors - rainy weather –
February 1996

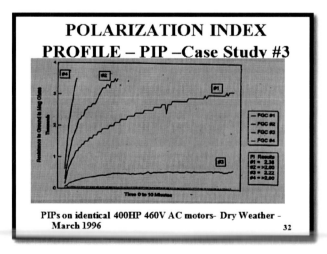

PIPs on identical 400HP 460V AC motors- Dry Weather -
March 1996

POLARIZATION INDEX
PROFILE – PIP – Case Study #4

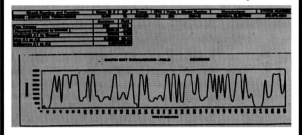

- **DC motor field PIP values varied from 0 to >3500 Meg Ohms**
- **After cleaning dipping and baking, readings stabilized at maximum (3500 Meg Ohms) for duration of 10 minute test**

33

Case Study: 400HP Bag House Fan Motor

Courtesy of PdMA Corporation - Noah Bethel
Used with Permission

- Unit has been in service for three (3) years
- Multiple drive failures since installation
- No root cause determined for failures
- Recent failure led to more extensive internal investigation - with no success
- Still no source found for the problem

34

PIP Case Study #4
Bag House Fan Assembly Motor

- AC Induction
- General Electric
- 400 Horsepower
- 1780 RPM
- 509LL Frame
- 460 Volt
- 442 FL Amps

35

400 HP Fan Motor Problem

- Four (4) Variable Frequency Drive failures within a short life span (all within 3 years)
- Electric Motor recently refurbished, but circuit initial RTG reading of only 145 Meg Ohms
- All other circuit data were in the normal range
- VFD's always replaced with new components at a cost of $45,000 each
- Frequent trips of the motor causing additional process problems

36

Polarization Index Test at Local Disconnect

Final value less than 400 Mohm

PI Test (#10 Baghouse Fan - Stator) 07/26/2003 09:29:23 AM

Erratic graph indicative of moisture and/or contamination

37

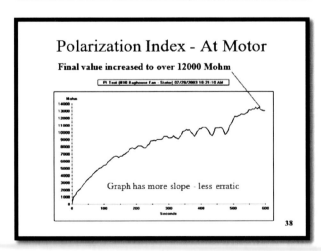

Polarization Index - At Motor

Final value increased to over 12000 Mohm

PI Test (#10 Baghouse Fan - Stator) 07/26/2003 10:21:10 AM

Graph has more slope - less erratic

38

Troubleshooting Actions

- **With motor RTG High and circuit RTG much lower, problem was suspected between local disconnect and the motor connection box**
- **Conduit was inspected for signs of moisture, but none was found initially**
- **Due to some abrasions on lead-wire jacket, it was decided to have it replaced**
- **As old wire was removed, water began leaking from jacket around it**

39

Root Cause of Low RTG

07 31 2003

- Unit has operated without trip since cable replaced

40

Step Voltage Testing
Typical Graph

41

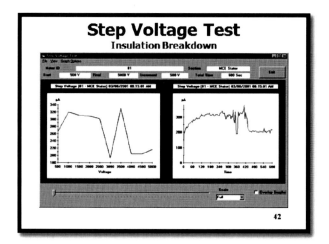

Step Voltage Test
Insulation Breakdown

42

Stator With Damaged Insulation

Burned insulation has been "Carbonized" making it
conductive and allowing current "leakage" directly to motor
frame components in contact with "ground" potential

43

Diagnostic Testing Using Light Probe

TEST LIGHT FOR OPENS AND GROUNDS
AC Dual Voltage Motors

- To find grounds, attach neutral to frame and line probe to one
  end of each sector – Light indicates ground in that sector
- To find opens, attach neutral & line probe to opposite ends of
  each sector – No light when open in that sector

44

Troubleshooting With a Light Probe

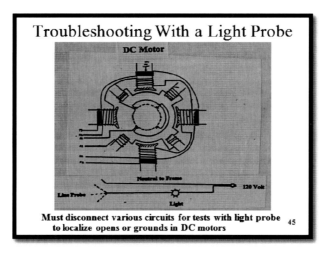

Must disconnect various circuits for tests with light probe to localize opens or grounds in DC motors 45

TROUBLESHOOTING WITH AMMETER

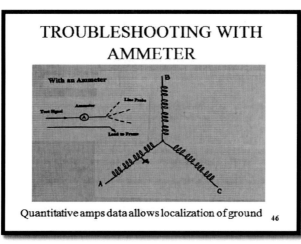

Quantitative amps data allows localization of ground 46

TROUBLESHOOTING WITH AMMETER

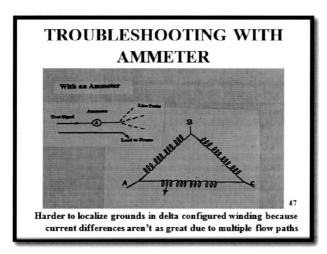

47

Harder to localize grounds in delta configured winding because current differences aren't as great due to multiple flow paths

Voltage Drop Test

- **May be used on DC motor field circuits or AC Synchronous motor rotors to find poles that are shorted**
  - **Decision to rewind or do minor repair depends on location of short, age of winding and time available before motor must be returned to service**
- **Either AC or DC voltage may be used, but AC gives the best indication (highest voltage drop per pole) with a small total voltage applied (~120 Volts in most cases)**

48

VOLTAGE DROP TEST

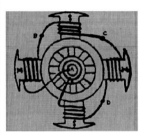

- Apply 120 V (AC) between slip rings
- Measure voltage between:
  - A & B
  - B & C
  - C & D
  - D & E
  - Pole with lowest voltage drop is weakest (worst short)
- All equal ⇒ Good condition

49

Bar-to-Bar Testing

- DC armatures suspected of having one or more coils shorted can be thoroughly tested using a quantitative bar-to-bar test.
- The test consists of using a milli-ohm or micro-ohmmeter to measure the resistance of each coil
- To obtain accurate readings, especially on large armatures where the resistance is quite low a special "four point probe" technique is used to eliminate effects of the resistance at the contact points of the probes on each bar
- All readings should be within about 10% of each other

50

Case Study: Armature Failure

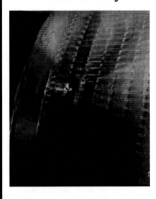

- **8000HP Aluminum Rougher Mill motor failed due to ground on armature**
- **Question was how soon and at what cost the motor could be returned to service**
- **Bar-to-Bar test was conducted to determine extent of damage**

51

Case Study: Armature Failure

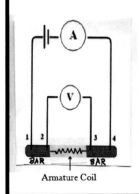

- **Bar-to bar test ordered to determine extent of damage to 2200 bar armature**

- **"Four Point Probe Pickup" required to measure extremely low resistance readings in the micro-ohm range**

52

Kelvin Probe Principles

Armature Coil

- Force connections (current leads 1 & 4) generate voltage drops across the resistance to be measured & across the force wires themselves.
- Sense connections (voltage leads 2 & 3) are made immediately adjacent to the target resistance.
- Accuracy of the technique comes from the fact that almost no current flows in the sense wires, so the voltage drop $V=IR$ is extremely low.

53

Case Study: Armature Failure

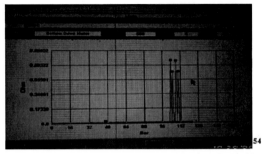

Spikes indicate that armature coils between about 100 & 112 are damaged. Ultimately a replacement was installed and the damaged armature was completely rewound for use as spare

Identifying Motor Defects Through Fault Zone Analysis

The six electric Fault Zones are:

1. Power Quality
2. Power Circuit
3. Insulation
4. Stator
5. Rotor
6. Air Gap

Fault Zone 1 - Power Quality

- Thrust in the limelight by utility deregulation and the popularity of AC and DC drives and other non-linear loads can significantly increasing the distortion levels of voltage and current
- Voltage and current harmonic distortion, voltage spikes, voltage unbalance and power factor are concerns when discussing power quality
- The presence of harmonics in a distribution system results in excessive heat from the increased current demands

Harmonic Distortion

- **Most common reference is Total Harmonic Distortion (THD) caused by non-linear loads such as computers, florescent lighting and variable speed drives (VSD's)**

- **THD is the ratio of the root-mean-square (RMS) of the harmonic content to the RMS value of the fundamental, expressed as a % of the fundamental**

- **A perfect 60 Hz sine wave would have 0% THD**

- **IEEE guidelines recommend <5% voltage THD & <3% individual harmonic distortion** 57

Unacceptable Levels of Voltage Distortion

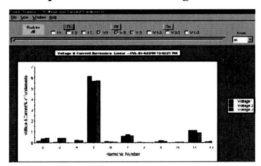

High 5th and 7th harmonics indicate the presence of a 6 pulse drive influence on the distribution system 58

6 Pulse VSD Pulses on Fundamental

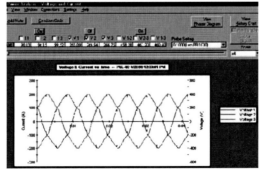

High harmonic levels can be seen on the voltage signal as pulses riding the fundamental freq. 59

Fault Zone 2 - Power Circuit

- Refers to all the conductors and connections that exist from the point at which the testing starts through to the connections at the motor
- Includes circuit breakers, fuses, contactors, overloads, disconnects, and lug connections.
- A good motor, although initially in perfect health, installed into a faulty power circuit causing temperatures to increase and insulation damage to occur
- Motor is replaced and the failure cycle begins again.

60

Mechanisms Causing High Resistance Connections

- Corroded terminals
- Loose cables
- Loose bus bars
- Corroded fuse clips
- Corroded contacts
- Open leads
- Different size conductors
- Dissimilar metals

61

NEMA Derating Curve from MG-1

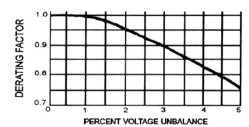

High resistance connections resulting in voltage imbalances will mandate reducing the horsepower rating significantly.

62

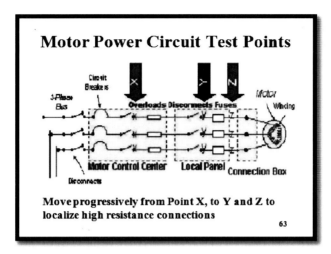

Motor Power Circuit Test Points

Move progressively from Point X, to Y and Z to localize high resistance connections

63

Fault Zone 3 - Insulation

- Refers to the insulation system between the winding conductors and ground
- Hazards to insulation life include heat caused by:
  - Power supply voltage unbalance, harmonics
  - Stress due to voltage spikes, inductive surges from breakers opening and closing
  - Operational overloading
  - Lightning strikes

64

Measured and Temperature Corrected RTG Readings Over Time

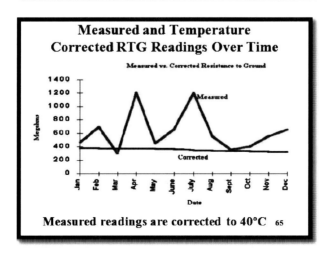

Measured readings are corrected to 40°C 65

Polarization Index Profile (PIP) Plot
PI = 1.94

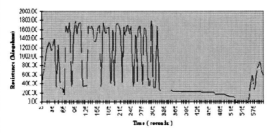

Always look at the Polarization Index Profile, and not just the Polarization Index ratio. 66

Fault Zone 4 - Stator

- Includes DC field or 3 phase AC windings, insulation between the turns of the windings, the stator or field pole core laminations and solder or brazed joints in conductors between the coils.
- Stators and DC field poles suffer:
  - Turn-to-turn faults, which can ultimately destroy winding effectiveness
  - Core damage by destroying insulation between laminations
- AC stators suffer phase-to-phase damage

67

RTG Isn't Enough!

- Testing with just a DC RTG tester for diagnosis may will identify many motor faults
  - Failure to find turn-to-turn or phase-to-phase shorts that haven't progresses to a ground fault may result in significantly more damage if motor is restarted
- Testing with high frequency (low current) AC signals in the conductor path phase-to-phase produces magnetic fields around the windings
  - Should be matched between phases if there is no imbalance caused by winding faults -
  - i.e., Inductive imbalance should equal zero 68

RTG Isn't Enough!

Hi-Frequency AC Test to
Locate Inductive Imbalance
on Wye Connected motor

Hi-Frequency AC Test to
Locate Inductive Imbalance
on DELTA Connected motor

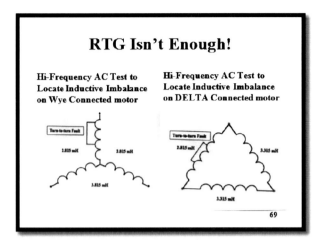

69

Fault Zone 5 - Rotor

- Refers to the bars, laminations and end or shorting rings of cage rotors
- Only ~10% of failures in motors occur here but they can affect other zones
  - Heat generated by rotor faults can destroy stator insulation and bearings repeatedly if rotor defects not found and corrected
- Rotor Influence Check (RIC) – an off-line test measures inductance in all phases with rotor in successive stationary positions of rotation
  - Magnetic coupling between rotor and stator affects inductance readings

70

Rotor Influence Check (RIC™)

Off-Line Test detects rotor
bars, cracked end rings or
damaged laminations

A normal rotor would have
no skewing or erratic
inductance patterns

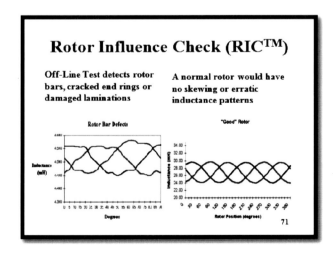

71

Fault Zone 6 – Air Gap

- An important feature that can affect motor performance
- If air gap is not evenly sustained at all times as the rotating element turns 360 degrees, uneven magnetic fields can be produced
- Magnetic imbalances can cause movement of windings, resulting in winding failure and electrically induced vibration resulting in bearing failure
- faulty relationship between the rotor and stator or armature and stationary field is an eccentricity. 72

Static & Dynamic Eccentricity

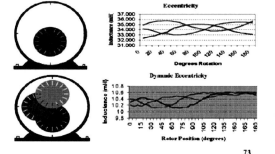

Conclusion Concerning Fault Zone Analysis

- Do not make quick decisions
- Look at the whole picture in a troubleshooting or diagnostic situation
- Break the system down into its individual fault zones, test each fault zone completely with every technology available to you
- Make your recommendations written or verbal using the terminology used in fault zone analysis to express your confidence and capabilities. 74

Chapter 7

Core and Growler Testing for Detection and Location of Motor Defects

Chapter 7
Motor Electrical Predictive Maintenance & Testing

1

Introduction

- Test method for core loss testing in repair shops developed in late 1970's & early 1980's when it became obvious that motor core damage could be a root cause of overheating & failure of winding insulation systems and in reducing motor efficiency

- Motor experts began advising on safe practices for winding removal before new winding installed.

•Repair Shop needed to avoid failures in warranty period

•Motor owners needed to avoid production delays due to failures

Burnout Oven
Temperature Monitor

2

Core, Core Loss or Loop Testing

- Test unit energizes the core (also referred to as back iron) to about 85,000 lines per square inch flux density using a low voltage, high current signal in a "loop" of cable that passes through core of a stator or pair of shaft clamps that pass current through a rotating assembly (rotor or armature)
- Test induces eddy currents and hysteresis in motor cores
- As a starting point, core tester algorithms use "watts per pound" data provided by "electrical" steel manufacturers as basis for comparison with actual reading from tester

3

Core Test of Stator

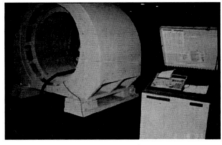

Set up for core test of large motor stator showing tester, (big) "loop" cable and (small) voltage sensor cable 4

Core Test Algorithms

- Computer algorithms or "curves" have been developed from a composite watts per pound data for a variety of most used "electrical" steel grades
  - Data have been adjusted for assembly into cores
- Core dimensions are entered to determine the actual power input required for the test

Core length	Total slot depth
Core diameter	Vent duct widths
Back Iron depth	Number of vent ducts

- For core dimensions, tester computer calculates watts or kilowatts per pound expected to be lost to eddy current generated heat

5

Core Test Computer

- Dimensions are inserted into the computer and it calculates the voltage needed to conduct the test.
- Current actually drawn when that voltage is reached determines watts or kilowatts per pound loss for condition assessment 6

Core Test of Rotor or Armature

Core test of small rotor or armature uses clamps to direct current for energizing eddy currents & hysteresis 7

Rotor Rigged for Core Test

8

TESTING CORE LAMINATIONS FOR SHORTS

- Used on cores of stators, rotors, armatures

- Low voltage, high current and frequency used to induce eddy currents and hysteresis in core

- Type of steel used in core along with core manufacturing methods and conditions determines "rating" used to establish test conditions and evaluate results

- Shorted or otherwise damaged laminations & core cause larger eddy currents & hysteresis & higher losses

9

- If losses are excessive, may have to repair or scrap core

Eddy Currents & Hysteresis

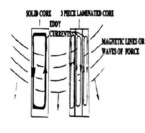

SOLID CORE   3 PIECE LAMINATED CORE

EDDY CURRENTS

MAGNETIC LINES OR WAVES OF FORCE

- Reducing thickness of core laminations reduces power loss from eddy currents by a factor of the square of the number laminations in the same volume

- Hysteresis loss results from energy used as molecules of iron are reversed by (alternating) current flowing in a motor

- Both produce heat, which is a threat to insulation and structural integrity of motor components

10

Core Design Factors Affecting Losses

- Core losses are affected by the following factors:
  - Lamination thickness – Most important factor
  - Lamination punching or stamping burrs
  - Lamination clamping pressure
  - Type of insulation coating used on steel
  - Heat treatment process used on punched laminations
  - Lamination assembly method
  - Silicon content and hardness of steel

11

Core Test Performance Criteria

- The computer will indicate for the core dimensions the level of voltage needed for the test and the number of amps that should be observed at that level
- Voltage is increased to the level specified and the actual amps flowing is compared to the calculated estimate
  - If lower than amps estimate => good core
  - If higher than amps estimate => some core damage

12

Core Hotspot Check

- As a final step in the Core Test procedure, the level of current is raised to two or three time the normal test amps for about one minute

- Using either a human hand or an infra red thermography instrument, hotspots are located and then marked with chalk or other harmless marking substance for correction

13

CORE TESTING
LAMINATIONS FOR SHORTS

- Under test conditions "hotspots" that indicate locations of shorts are easily detected by feeling core with hands or scanning with an infra red instrument   14

Core Condition Evaluation

- **Core Loss algorithm used to calculate:**
  - Watts per pound
    - Compares this to "Good" "Marginal" and "Bad" Ranges: 2-5 w/#
      =>Good 6-8w/# =>Marginal >8=>Bad – Range runs to 10
  - Apparent Power Factor - Watts/Current x Voltage
    - Range 0.2 to 0.9 Lower=>Good - Higher => Bad
  - Ampere-Turns per inch (AT/IN)
    - Range 0 to 26 - Lower is better
  - Computer compares AT/IN to composite of published curves of AT/IN vs. Flux Density used for evaluation over many years for core testing and found to be accurate for >90% of new and old cores tested
  - Computer then indicates actual flux in lines per inch

15

Typical Report of Core Condition

- **Input data: Date; Job #; Core Length (inches) Core Depth (inches) Back Iron (inches), Total Slot Depth (inches); Width of Vent Ducts (inches) and Total Number of Vents**
- **Computed setup data: Volts; Approximate Amps; Approximate Watts**
- **Measured data: Actual Volts, Amps & Watts**
- **Recommendations & results:**
  - Example for bad core: Core loss too high! Take corrective steps and retest or reject.
  - For all (Good, Marginal & Bad) gives: Measured Watts per pound, AT/IN, AT/IN from experience curves (along with maximum value in range of each) and Flux Density

16

Relative Comparison of Core Loss Data

- **Because of the nature of the measurement and calculation of core loss and the assumptions and generalization of multiple source data into a set of "curves" the best method evaluating core loss data is to:**
  - Compare core loss data when the motor is new to core loss data when the motor is received in the shop for repair
    - Should be the same with and without winding installed
  - Compare core loss data from before the removal of the winding to that from after removal using any heating or mechanical method or combination thereof
    - Any increase implies the probability that motor will not be as efficient when placed back into service

17

Core Hotspot Correction

- Variety of tools used to eliminate hotspots
  - Plastic or hard rubber hammer (to pound on core ends to "crack" it
  - Hammer and sharpened hack saw blade to separate laminations welded at the surface
  - Insulating spray that may be applied between separated laminations
  - Grinders for removing the surfaces of laminations that have been "peened over"

18

Core Hotspot Correction

19

Using a sharpened hacksaw blade to separate core laminations is effective most times in eliminating hot spots in motor cores

Core Hotspot Correction

20

Worst case, when a replacement isn't immediately available, a motor core must be re-cored either with new or refurbished laminations. This is not uncommon for older, large motors

Core Testing Case Study

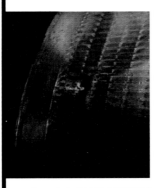

- Commonwealth Aluminum Rolling Mill drive motor armature winding failed to ground during full load operation
- Spare was available and was installed
- Root cause found to be poor quality control of last armature rewind 5 years earlier
- Rewind ordered

21

Core Test Case Study

- Close up of major damage shows laminations apparently in tact
- Question of whether inter-laminar insulation was damaged was resolved favorably by core test prior to rewind

22

Avoiding Increased Core Loss and Decreased Efficiency

- Ensure that when ordering motor winding replacement that old winding removal is done under closely controlled conditions
  - Limit "burn-out" oven temperature
    - ➤ 680°F (360°C) for laminations with organic coating
    - ➤ 750°F (400°C) for laminations with inorganic coating
    - ➤ Lower temperatures doesn't always soften insulation materials sufficiently to "clean" the core when conductors are removed
  - Ensure mechanical tools used to remove old winding coils do not damage core laminations   23

Alternative Core Test Method

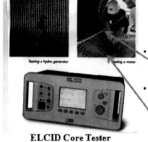

ELCID Core Tester

- Portable device called ELCID can be taken into the field for core testing small sections of a large motor stator or rotor core (or generator component cores)
- An excitation loop through the core of with rotor removed is energized
- Core tester sensor (Chottock Potentiometer Coil) is positioned across a section of core to detect magnetic field of the eddy currents induced by the excitation loop

24

Core Energizing Loop

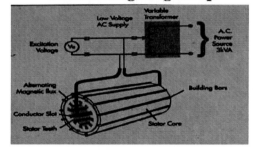

Core is energized to produce eddy currents in manner similar to other core tests

25

Motor Core Test Sensor

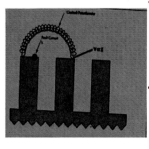

- Chottock Potentiometer is used to sense magnetic fields produced by eddy currents induced to flow in the core
- Larger-than-normal (fault) eddy currents are caused by damaged laminations and show on tester screen as voltage variation proportional to current 26

Motor Core Test Signals

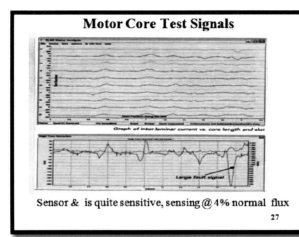

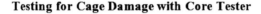

Sensor & is quite sensitive, sensing @ 4% normal flux

27

Testing for Cage Damage with Core Tester

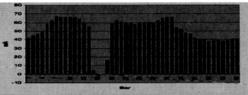

- ADWEL International Ltd for many years sold a unit called the Motor Core Tester
- It operates on Chottoch Potentiometer Sensing principles and many are still in use
- Screen shot above from a results of testing a 46 bar cage rotor (at least 4 bad bars)

28

Growlers

- Basically a coil of wire wrapped around a laminated iron core – a half transformer
  - Come in various sizes from hand held to bench mounted or separately mounted on a rolling frame
  - Typically energized with single phase 115-120 Volt 60 Hz or 220-240 Volt 50 Hz power found in shop
  - Used to energize conductors of motor components by "transformer action" in conjunction with a thin steel strip (like a hack saw blade) to reveal shorts
  - Many are "home made" but commercial versions are available

29

GROWLER TESTING

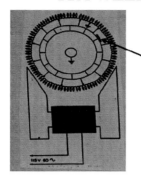

- Induces current flow by transformer action if circuit to ground present
- Location found using hack saw blade, metal ruler or thin steel strip or "growls" as it vibrates
  - Sparks on commutator bars indicates shorts in coils connected to these bars
  - Steel strip vibrates when passed over shorted coil(s)
- Works for Wave Wound, **not** Lap Wound with cross connected (equalized) coils
  - Vibration occurs at every slot

30

Growler and Magnetic Sheet Testing

- Growler & magnetic sheet test to find defective rotor bars
- Open bars will **not** show alignment of particles in sheet above the affected bar

31

Growler Testing Large Squirrel Cage Rotor

Growler is the object on top of the rotor which is inducing current to flow in the cage, aligning particles in the sheets

32

Growler Testing Stator Winding for Shorts

- With rotor removed:
  - Place a growler on bottom of stator interior and energize it to cause "transformer action" in the winding
    - Move it around the circumference of the stator, slot to slot
  - Place a hack saw blade or thin steel strip close to the core aligned to the axis of the rotor on the other side of the coil being energized
  - The blade will vibrate if a short is located in a particular coil

33

APPENDIX D

Motor Electrical Predictive Maintenance & Testing Seminar Text

Bibliography

(List of References Recommended for Motor Program Managers)

The publications listed herein are recommended for inclusion in your library. Web sites should be added to your "favorites" list to be referred to in support of an active motor management program. Studying and following the guidelines provided in what's listed below (along with what's in this seminar text) will result in a world class motor management program.

Electrical Insulation (Bi-monthly) Magazine and the **Transactions on Dielectrics and Electrical Insulation, Dielectrics & Electrical Insulation Society of the IEEE** www.ieee.com (Comes with membership in IEEE and selection of this society within it. Recommended for those seriously needing in-depth understanding of insulation and dielectrics principles and new developments in research on the subject.)

Electric Motor Repair 1986 Robert Rosenberg & August Hand, ISBN 0-03-059584-3 This book should be a "must" for anyone involved with motor repair. Available through www.directtextbook.com (check price comparisons from different sources) Check for availability of used copies of this book at www.alibris.com

Electrical Apparatus (Monthly) Magazine, Barks Publications, Inc., 400N Michigan Ave, Chicago, IL 60611 4198

www.eamagazine.com or www.barks.com (This is a must! Free subscription may be available for qualified applicants.)

Electrical Insulation for Rotating Machine Design, Evaluation, Aging, Testing & Repair 2003 Greg Stone et. al. ISBN –0-471-445096- www.wiley.com The authors were on the team that developed Handbook to Assess the Insulation Condition of Large Rotating Machines (Volume 16 of the Power Plant Reference Series) published in 1989 and 1991 by Electric Power Research Institute (EPRI), but limited in distribution largely to EPRI members.

Energy Efficient Motor Systems, A Handbook on Technology , Program, and Policy Opportunities Second Edition 2002 Steven Nadel, et. al., American Council for an Energy Efficient Economy, Washington, DC www.aceee.org (motors book page)

Managing Controls 1993 Richard Nailen, P.E. Barks Publications, Inc., 400N Michigan Ave, Chicago, IL 60611 4198 ISBN 0-943876-06-0 www.barks.com. Prepared by Engineering Editor of Electrical Apparatus Magazine

Managing Motors, 2nd Edition 1996 Richard Nailen, P.E. Barks Publications, Inc., 400N Michigan Ave, Chicago, IL 60611 4198 ISBN 0-943876-09-5 www.barks.com. Prepared by Engineering Editor of Electrical Apparatus Magazine and editor of the Volume 6 of the Power Plant Reference Series, Motors, for Electric Power Research Institute in the mid-1980's

Motor Circuit Analysis: Theory, Application and Energy Analysis, Penrose, Howard W, Ph.D., Success by Design Publishing, 2001. This is a must for anyone involved with motor testing written by one of the most influential individuals in the motor testing and diagnostic field.

Practical Guide to Troubleshooting, Installation and Maintenance of Variable Frequency Drives 2001, EC&M Books, Intertec Publishing, 9800 Metcalf Avenue Overland Park Kansas, 66212-2215 www.ecmweb.com Short, easily understood essentials on VFD/VSDs.

Standard Handbook for Electrical Engineers 14th Edition 1999 edited by Donald G. Fink & H Wayne Beaty, McGraw-Hill

Publishers, NY, NY ISBN 0-7022005-0 Check www.fetchbooks.info and compare prices from the sources listed at that site for new and used copies.

In addition to the web sites listed above for purchase of publications the following provide numerous documents and some software programs that pertain to the subject of motor purchase, maintenance, testing, repair. Most are free for download and some sites have items for sale, as indicated.

www.advancedenergy.com Free download of "Guidelines for Good Motor Repair" and other documents in their "Knowledge Library."

www.alltestpro.com has many free downloadable articles, case studies and technical notes available for download.

www.cee1.org Consortium for Energy Efficiency is developing a "Motor Systems Tool Kit" some parts of which are now available for free download. There are links to other useful web sites, like the ones listed below

www.easa.com Numerous documents on motor repair and maintenance as well as training videos, CD's and DVD's on motor repair and related subject are for sale (Members of the Electrical Apparatus Service Association –EASA get substantial discounts on all items).

www.irispower.com & www.adwel.com (Information Vault) Many case studies and technical papers are available for free download. A newsletter is also available from this organization.

www.maintenance-tips.com has an e-mail newsletter to which you can subscribe and an archive of maintenance tips on many subjects, including motor testing. There are also links to case studies and papers on motors.

www.motorsmatter.org Web site sponsored by DOE and many commercial motor suppliers has many items for free download, as well as links to the sponsors' and other useful web sites.

www.oit.doe.gov/bestpractices Many downloadable documents on best practices for motors and systems that use motors from the Department of Energy Office of Industrial Technology – All are free.

www.pdma.com has many free downloadable articles, case studies customer success stories on on-line and off-line motor testing and links to other useful sites.

www.reliabilityweb.com has an enormous amount of data on maintenance and reliability and a growing number of free downloadable items of interest to motor program managers. There are over 100 links to other sites, many involving motors.

INDEX

Motor Electrical Predictive Maintenance & Testing Volume 2

JACK R. NICHOLAS, JR., P.E. (California – Quality Branch), CMRP (since 2001) BS (General Engineering from U.S. Naval Academy), MBA (The American University of Washington, D.C.), Graduate of the Navy Nuclear Propulsion Officer Training Program and Captain, USNR (Retired) has 52 years experience in operation, maintenance, monitoring and teaching about electric motors, small generators and related systems and components on assets such as nuclear powered submarines, nuclear and fossil powered electrical generation facilities, manufacturing plants and commercial facilities in North America, Europe, Asia, Australia, and the Caribbean.

For 17 years (1971-1988), as a civil service senior engineer, he was involved with an initiative to extend the operating and life cycles of nuclear subs. After early retirement from civil service in 1988, Mr. Nicholas was hired by Halliburton Corporation to develop a predictive condition monitoring capability for application in its oil field and petro-chemical industry services subsidiaries. This led to acquisition of Precision Mechanical Analysis (PMA) Inc, of Tampa, FL , where he supported development of a new Lubricant and Wear Particle Analysis Laboratory and conceived and supported research and development of an off-line electrical motor test suite named the Motor Circuit Evaluation (MCE) Tester. PMA became known as PdMA, during that time. PdMA was sold by Halliburton to a private investor in 1993 and became PdMA Inc. Mr. Nicholas, as PdMA Inc., Senior VP, became deeply involved with commercial introduction of the MCE Tester in the USA, Canada and Australia. He developed a training course and associated classroom text to teach motor basic theory and MCE testing, which was the precursor to this publication. In 1996 Mr. Nicholas left PdMA and with his wife formed Maintenance Quality Systems (MQS) LLC. He retained rights to the training materials he had developed and began expansion of the "Motor Electrical Predictive Maintenance and Testing" text and course materials to include all commercially available methods for assessment and monitoring of motors of all sizes (and small generators), along with many related subjects.

GEOFF GENERALOVIC is a senior maintenance electrician with 38 years heavy industry experience, the last 17 as a company- wide Predictive Maintenance practitioner at ArcelorMittleDofasco Inc., in Hamilton, Ontario, Canada. He started at Dofasco as a general repair electrician in 1973 working in different business units. In 1993 was assigned to a newly formed Process Maintenance Team (PMT) in the company's Hot Strip Rolling Mill business unit. Eventually, he moved from the PMT to the Predictive Maintenance (PdM) group. Today Geoff is part of the company's central PdM team and is using his skills plant- wide in ten (10) different production business units. Geoff is also an experienced trainer, providing infrared courses under FLIR sponsorship in Canada that are open to the public. He is involved with the Hamilton, Ontario Chapter of the Society for Maintenance and Reliability Professionals (SMRP)

He holds a Level III infrared thermography certification, using Agema and FLIR infrared cameras. He is certified in its use. He also routinely uses AREVA's EMPATH on-line motor circuit tester. Geoff has a Level I Ultrasonics certification and has had basic vibration training. As part of his training he has presented professional papers at various maintenance and reliability conferences sponsored by The Snell Group, the Association for Iron and Steel Technology, P/PM Technology Magazine, PdMA Corporation, and ReliabilityWeb.com. Participation as co-author of "Motor Electrical Predictive Maintenance and Testing" text is his first attempt at writing a book.

About Reliabilityweb.com

Created in 1999, Reliabilityweb.com provides educational information and peer-to-peer networking opportunities that enable safe and effective maintenance reliability and asset management for organizations around the world.

Activities include:

Reliabilityweb.com (www.reliabilityweb.com) includes educational articles, tips, video presentations, an industry event calendar and industry news. Updates are available through free email subscriptions and RSS feeds. **Confiabilidad.net** is a mirror site that is available in Spanish at www.confiabilidad.net

Uptime Magazine (www.uptimemagazine.com) is a bi-monthly magazine launched in 2005 that is highly prized by the maintenance reliability and asset management community. Editions are obtainable in print, online, digital, Kindle and through the iPad/iPhone app.

Reliability Performance Institute Conferences and Training Events (www.maintenanceconference.com) offer events that range from unique, focused-training workshops and seminars to small focused conferences to large industry-wide events, including the International Maintenance Conference, RELIAbIlIty 2.0 and Solutions 2.0.

MRO-Zone Bookstore (www.mro-zone.com) is an online bookstore offering a maintenance reliability and asset management focused library of books, DVDs and CDs published by Reliabilityweb.com and other leading publishers, such as Industrial Press, McGraw-Hill, CRC Press and more.

Association for Maintenance Professionals (www.maintenance.org) is a member organization and online community that encourages professional development and certification and supports information exchange and learning with 10,000+ members worldwide.

A Word About Social Good

Reliabilityweb.com is mission driven to deliver value and social good to the maintenance reliability and asset management communities. Doing good work and making profit is not inconsistent, and as a result of Reliabilityweb.com's mission-driven focus, financial stability and success has been the outcome. For over a decade, Reliabilityweb.com's positive contributions and commitment to the maintenance reliability and asset management communities have been unmatched.

Other causes Reliabilityweb.com has financially contributed to include industry associations, such as SMRP, AFE, STLE, ASME and ASTM, and community charities, including the Salvation Army, American Red Cross, Wounded Warrior Project, Paralyzed Veterans of America and the Autism Society of America. In addition, we are proud supporters of our U.S. Troops and first responders who protect our freedoms and way of life. That is only possible by being a for-profit company that pays taxes.

I hope you will get involved with and explore the many resources that are available to you through the Reliabilityweb.com network.

Warmest regards,
Terrence O'Hanlon
CEO, Reliabilityweb.com

uptime® Elements™

A Reliability System For Asset Performance Management

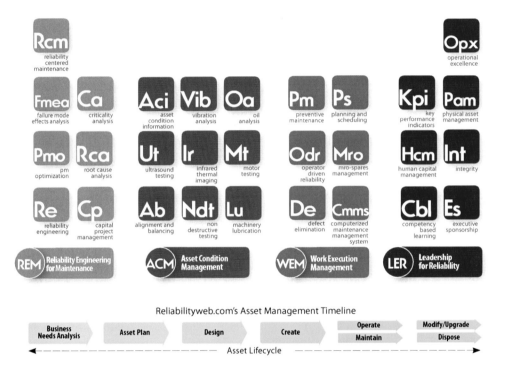

Reliabilityweb.com's Asset Management Timeline

Business Needs Analysis | Asset Plan | Design | Create | Operate / Maintain | Modify/Upgrade / Dispose

Asset Lifecycle

Uptime Elements are a trademark of Uptime Magazine • ©2014 Uptime Magazine uptimemagazine.com • reliabilityweb.com • maintenance.org

Reliabilityweb.com® and Uptime® Magazine Mission: **To make the people we serve safer and more successful.**
One way we support this mission is to suggest a reliability system for asset performance management as pictured above.
Our use of the Uptime Elements is designed to assist you in categorizing and organizing your own Body of Knowledge (BoK) whether it be through training, articles, books or webinars. Our hope is to make YOU safer and more successful.